A Second Level Course

STUDY GUIDE 4

ISSUES IN WOMEN'S STUDIES

Prepared for the Course Team by
Richard Allen, Frances Bonner,
Lizbeth Goodman and Catherine King

THE OPEN UNIVERSITY U207 *ISSUES IN WOMEN'S STUDIES* COURSE PRODUCTION TEAM

Amanda Willett, Barbara Hodgson, Catherine King (Chair), Diana Gittins, Dinah Birch, Felicity Edholm, Fiona Harris, Frances Bonner, Gill Kirkup, Harry Dodd, Helen Crowley, Joan Mason, Judy Lown, Kathryn Woodward, Laurie Smith Keller, Linda Janes, Linda McDowell, Lizbeth Goodman, Maggie Riley, Maureen Adams, Meg Sheffield, Melanie Bayley, Randhir Auluck, Richard Allen, Rosemary Pringle, Siân Lewis, Susan Crosbie, Susan Himmelweit, Susan Khin Zaw, Tony Coulson, Veronica Beechey, Wendy Webster

External Assessor: Elizabeth Wilson, Professor of Policy Studies, Polytechnic of North London

The Open University
Walton Hall
Milton Keynes MK7 6AB

First published 1992

Copyright © 1992 The Open University

All rights reserved. No part of this publication may be reproduced, stored in a retrieval system, or transmitted, in any form or by any means, without written permission from the publisher or a licence from the Copyright Licensing Agency Limited. Details of such licences (for reprographic reproduction) may be obtained from the Copyright Licensing Agency Ltd of 33–34 Alfred Place, London WC1E 7DP.

Designed by the Graphic Design Group of The Open University

Printed and bound in the United Kingdom by Staples Printers Rochester Limited, Neptune Close, Medway City Estate, Frindsbury, Rochester, Kent ME2 4LT.

ISBN 0 7492 0106 1

This publication forms part of the Open University course U207 *Issues in Women's Studies*. If you have not enrolled on the course and would like to buy this and other Open University material, please write to Open University Educational Enterprises Ltd, 12 Cofferidge Close, Stony Stratford, Milton Keynes MK11 1BY, United Kingdom. If you wish to enquire about enrolling as an Open University student, please write to the Central Enquiry Office, The Open University, P.O. Box 200, Walton Hall, Milton Keynes MK7 2YZ, United Kingdom.

1.1

Cover illustration by Christine Tacq

4294C/u207sg4i1.1

CONTENTS

	Introduction	5
	Aims	6
	Timetabling	7
	Structure of this Study Guide	8
1	**Book Four Introduction (Week 24)**	9
2	**Chapter 1 Themes and issues: gender, genre and representation (Weeks 24–25)**	10
	Article 1.1 'Making things mean' by Catherine King	12
	Set book: *Wayward Girls and Wicked Women*	14
	Article 1.2 'Analysing representations' by Richard Allen	14
	Article 1.3 'Gender and genre' by Dinah Birch	19
	Article 1.4 'Ways of speaking' by Joan Swann	21
3	**Chapter 2 Literary representations: self as subject (Weeks 26–27)**	24
	Literary representations: self as subject	25
	Chapter 2 introduction	25
	Article 2.1 'The feminist critical revolution' by Elaine Showalter	26
	Article 2.2 'Supply and demand: women's short stories' by Lizbeth Goodman	30
	Article 2.3 'Towards a better way of being: feminist science fiction' by Frances Bonner	36
	Summary	39
	Article 2.4 'A wild surmise: motherhood and poetry' by Alicia Ostriker	39
	Article 2.5 'Moment of faith: worksheets' by Carol Rumens	39
	Summary of key points about poetry	45
	Set book: *On Earth to Make the Numbers Up*	45
	Article 2.6 'Criticism as autobiography' by Nicole Ward Jouve	46
	Article 2.7 'Our lives: working-class women's autobiography in Britain' by Wendy Webster	46
	Summary	48
4	**Chapter 3 Visual images: taking the mastery out of art (Week 28)**	50
	Chapter 3 introduction	51
	Article 3.1 'The politics of representation: a democracy of the gaze' by Catherine King	53
	Article 3.2 'Object into subject: some thoughts on the work of black women artists' by Michelle Cliff	57

	Article 3.3 'Beyond the mirror: women's self portraits' by Felicity Edholm	58
	Article 3.4 'Feminist arts' by Catherine King	61
5	**Chapter 4 Negotiating meanings from popular television and film (Week 29)**	**68**
	Chapter 4 introduction	68
	Article 4.1 'Pleasurable negotiations' by Christine Gledhill	71
	Article 4.2 '*She's Gotta Have It:* the representation of black female sexuality on film' by Felly Nkweto Simmonds	73
	Article 4.3 'A woman's space: women and soap opera' by Christine Geraghty	75
	Article 4.4 'Confession time: women and game shows' by Frances Bonner	79
6	**Chapter 5 Pornography and representation (Week 30)**	**82**
	Chapter 5 introduction	82
	Article 5.1 '*Lace*: pornography for women?' by Avis Lewallen	84
	Article 5.2 'Obscenity and censorship' by Suzanne Kappeler	85
	Article 5.3 'Pornography and black women's bodies' by Patricia Hill Collins	86
	Article 5.4 'Who watches the watchwomen?: Feminists Against Censorship' by Gillian Rodgerson and Linda Semple	87
	Article 5.5 'The pornography problem' by Lizbeth Goodman	90
	Conclusion	91
7	**Chapter 6 Comic subversions (Week 30)**	**94**
	Beginning your study of comic subversions	94
	Article 6.1 'Gender and humour' by Lizbeth Goodman	100
	Article 6.2 'Comic subversions: comedy as strategy in feminist theatre' by Lizbeth Goodman	104
	Summary	105
8	**Book Four Conclusion (Week 30)**	**106**
	Poetry Supplement	108
	References	109
	Acknowledgements	109

INTRODUCTION

This Study Guide corresponds to the fourth major block of U207. Various forms of literary, artistic and popular cultural forms of representation will be studied, all in relation to the common theme of gender. You will have a fair amount of reading to do during the next seven weeks, and there are a number of ideas to keep in mind throughout.

Book Four, *Imagining Women: cultural representations and gender*, is the main text which you will be studying. This Study Guide has been designed to help you with the planning of your work, and to facilitate your understanding of the material you will encounter in *Imagining Women*. It should also help you to plan your reading of the two set books – Angela Carter's *Wayward Girls and Wicked Women* and Evelyn Haythorne's *On Earth to Make the Numbers Up* – which are integral, either in part or in entirety, to this block of the course. A Poetry Supplement is also provided. This has been designed to compliment the readings in all four books, but is particularly relevant to *Imagining Women*. In addition to these materials, this part of the course has been enriched with a number of broadcasts and audio-cassettes. This Study Guide will help you to make the best use of all these materials in studying and revising.

The forms of cultural representation examined in this block are quite diverse. They range from poetry, fiction and autobiography; to photographs and paintings; to soap operas, game shows and film; to different forms of pornography; to stand-up comedy and theatre. Issues of class and race difference are important in these areas of work, and are discussed in several of the readings in *Imagining Women*. In all these forms of cultural representations, the issue of women's active involvement in representing themselves through creative work in the arts, and through active participation in interpretation and analysis of those art forms, is addressed. Throughout the Study Guide, as in *Imagining Women*, the primary concern is the issue of gender as it intersects with women's representations and representations of women.

AIMS

The aims of this Study Guide are twofold:

1   To help you to organize your study of the many different written and broadcast/audio elements of the materials in this block.

2   To highlight important themes running throughout each article in *Imagining Women*, and to identify ways of making connections between parts of the book and major course themes.

The aims of this Study Guide are, in short, to support and facilitate your study of *Imagining Women* and the other set texts for this part of the course. The aims of *Imagining Women* are more specific. They include:

1   To identify different genres or forms of cultural representations and to study them as 'texts' produced and analysed within given cultural contexts.

2   To do so with reference to the gender of authors and audiences, writers and readers, artists and critical spectators.

3   To trace connections between women's roles as creators and interpreters of written texts, visual images and mediated representations of various kinds, including live performance.

4   To consider the implications in everyday life of all these forms of cultural representations. That is, to ask the following questions: how do they affect the way we see women, the way we represent women in our own writing, the way we see ourselves and our relationships with the images which bombard us in the modern world?

5   To offer some possible answers to such questions, but also to emphasize the difficulty of finding any single definitive answers, given the diversity of women and men who are our audience of readers (the students of U207).

TIMETABLING

Your work on *Imagining Women* is spread over seven weeks: Study Weeks 24–30 inclusive. During this time you will also be asked to read the whole of one set book, Evelyn Haythorne's *On Earth to Make the Numbers Up*, and several of the stories from the other set book, Angela Carter's *Wayward Girls and Wicked Women*. In addition, you will be asked to read the Poetry Supplement – a skim read at first, in connection with your work on Chapter 2, and then again as the final exercise at the end of this Study Guide.

Imagining Women is divided into six chapters, together with an Introduction and Conclusion. We recommend that you spend two weeks on the book introduction and Chapter 1 together, a further two weeks on Chapter 2, one week each on Chapters 3 and 4, reading Chapters 5 and 6 and the Conclusion in the final week, according to the timetable below. However, this timetable is for guidance only and you may find that you need to spend more or less time on certain parts of the book – in which case, we suggest that you adjust your workload accordingly.

Study Week	Chapter	Articles	Other Work
(22)			(Radio 08 Writing from the margins)
24 and 25	Introduction 1: Themes and issues: gender, genre and representation	Bonner and Goodman 1.1: King 1.2: Allen 1.3: Birch 1.4: Swann	Radio 09 Sisters in crime TV 07 Outside in: women artists and cultural difference
26 and 27	2: Literary representations: self as subject	2.1: Showalter 2.2: Goodman 2.3: Bonner 2.4: Ostriker 2.5: Rumens 2.6: Ward Jouve 2.7: Webster	TMA 06
28	3: Visual images: taking the mastery out of art	3.1: King 3.2: Cliff 3.3: Edholm 3.4: King	Radio 10 Feminist theatre
29	4: Negotiating meanings from popular television and film	4.1: Gledhill 4.2: Simmonds 4.3: Geraghty 4.4: Bonner	TV 08 Taking the credit: women in TV
30	5: Pornography and representation 6: Comic subversions Conclusion	5.1: Lewallen 5.2: Kappeler 5.3: Collins 5.4: Rodgerson and Semple 5.5: Goodman 6.1: Goodman 6.2: Goodman Walker	Poetry Supplement
(31)			(Radio 11 Women comics: satire and self image)

STRUCTURE OF THIS STUDY GUIDE

As *Imagining Women* and this corresponding Study Guide make up the last of the four major blocks of the course, they have been written in part as a response to the previous three. This does not mean that you should expect suddenly to find hidden answers to all the questions raised in the earlier books and Study Guides; rather, this part of the course addresses issues raised throughout the course from a different perspective. Most importantly, this block on 'Cultural Representations and Gender' emphasizes your role in the interpretive process which is part of any kind of study, but which is particularly relevant in women's studies.

The Study Guide is divided into eight sections: one for each chapter of *Imagining Women*, and one each for the Introduction and Conclusion. For each week's work, we have outlined key points and ideas which should serve to focus your reading of *Imagining Women* and the other set texts. Each article in *Imagining Women* is introduced and discussed briefly, often with a set of questions or concepts which are particularly important as major themes of the course. Some of the sections include activities of various kinds, all of which have been designed to increase your active participation in and understanding of this part of the course.

1
BOOK FOUR INTRODUCTION
(WEEK 24)
(prepared by Frances Bonner)

We would like you to read the introduction to Book Four, *Imagining Women*, before you study any of the individual articles, because it talks about the positions from which the book was constructed. One aspect foregrounded by the introduction that you will probably not have considered explicitly before is the question of the situated perspective of the writer and the acknowledgement of this in the language in which she (or he) writes. Think back to the articles you have been reading over the last month or so. Can you recall the pronouns used by the writers? Did they refer to themselves at all? Do you remember being taught at school to write 'properly'? Do you recall being told that masculine pronouns were impersonal and included reference to women?

We are not suggesting that you, or any writer, should overuse 'I', 'me' or 'my' – it is all too easy to sound like an egomaniac – or that you should regularly announce your gender, age, race, sexuality and so on prior to arguing a point. We are, however, arguing that constant use of 'impersonal' language is a device to hide and deny difference, as it has long hidden and denied women's experiences and perspectives.

You will already be familiar with arguments about essentialism from previous work on the course, but you should note any new inflection the term seems to have here as preparation for encountering it in the readings to come. The question of women's or feminist 'ways of seeing' is particularly important and you may want to re-read the relevant sections of this introduction as you progress through the book.

A third area of particular importance at this stage is the question of the relative power of the creator of representations and the critical audience. Much of the work you will be doing over the next seven weeks will involve asking you as members of a critical audience to take the power to create your own readings of particular representations. Reference to Jill Dolan's work on pages 6–7 of the book is a reminder that this may involve something of a loss for the creators. For example, the readings of Jean Fraser's photograph *Celestial Bodies* used in the next section of this Study Guide may well be very different from those she had in mind in creating it for a book on lesbian photography.

We are not, however, suggesting that *any* reading is possible, rather that a process of negotiation (discussed at length in Article 4.1 by Christine Gledhill) is entered into. Most of the work you have been doing in the course so far has involved you in working at two levels with critical and analytical material both in the books and in the commentary on them in the Study Guides. Often during the next seven weeks, you will be working on three levels with a text (such as a short story or a reproduction of a piece of visual art), criticism or analysis of this in the book and then the Study Guide commentary. This should make you particularly aware of the processes by which you make meanings from texts and the ways in which feminist creators and readers can work to transform representations of women.

2
CHAPTER 1 THEMES AND ISSUES: GENDER, GENRE AND REPRESENTATION (WEEKS 24 AND 25)
(prepared by Richard Allen)

Your work on Chapter 1 of *Imagining Women* is scheduled to take two weeks. Within this period we have allowed time for you to begin the reading required for Chapter 2, particularly the two set books: Evelyn Haythorne's autobiography *On Earth to Make the Numbers Up* and the stories from Angela Carter's *Wayward Girls and Wicked Women*.

At a number of points you should feel that your work on Chapter 1 touches on ideas you have encountered elsewhere in the course, particularly in Book One, *Knowing Women*. The discussions here differ in placing those ideas – subjectivity, psychoanalysis, the symbolic order, power, patriarchy – within the framework of 'culture' and the 'arts' and specific pieces of writing, painting and so on. The use of quotation marks here around 'culture' and 'arts' indicates from the beginning that these are words we do not want to take for granted as easy to understand and define. Throughout, we want you to question what these words mean. Catherine King does this in the first essay, stressing how definitions have emerged through time, and how 'art' has become almost entirely linked with what we should rather call 'high art'.

Using 'high' here raises another of the topics of this part of Book Four, namely the way language and all of the different media from which art may be made contain coding systems with messages embedded in them. Sometimes this can be very evident as when we read fairy tales or notice that a particular detail stands out in isolation in a picture, but at other times the codes and messages are quite suppressed and the language appears entirely familiar. Part of the study of art and culture involves removing this familiarity and seeing things not as natural but as strange. These codes are seldom only used in just one particular picture or piece of writing; rather, they are part of the wider patterns of coding systems, or of the various discourses, that are used within a culture.

In this respect, meanings of all kinds depend upon the contexts in which they arise. This is a key issue in Book Four and something the authors want you to see operating at a wide range of levels. When we read an obscure poem we may feel we need someone to provide a context and explain the meaning of words and phrases before we can understand it; at the other extreme, even the simplest act of communication depends on context – the words 'how are you?' spoken by one close friend to another have a different meaning when they are spoken by a member of the Royal Family to someone they encounter when opening a new building.

Another example of coding can be seen in the use of 'high' in the phrase 'high art', used to describe that art which is publicly recognized, collected in museums, galleries and libraries. 'High' here implies something near to the top of a scale. But it is characteristic of most of this art that it has a minority appeal – if one shifted to the phrase 'élite art' a different meaning would occur not only because 'élite' has a different meaning from 'high' in simple terms, but because the words carry different coded messages. If one shifted to 'rich people's art' then the coding and the meaning would be different again.

One response to the sense that conventional notions of high art were restricting has been the development of another field of study – 'popular culture'. We may then find ourselves discussing whether something is 'high art'

CHAPTER 1 THEMES AND ISSUES: GENDER, GENRE AND REPRESENTATION

or 'popular culture' and in doing so we juggle two codes – one in which something is high up a scale and one in which, apparently more democratically, 'popular' is a term of praise. Neither seems able to contain the other code's substantive word – so one speaks of 'art', the other of 'culture' – even though both words seem to mean the opposite of something which is natural and unformed.

Throughout this part of Book Four, it is argued that 'art' which is publicly recognized has been 'men's art' – a world and a coding system which has simply not recognized women's creativity either within conventional forms or specifically women's forms. Given this, it is inevitable that disruption figures largely in this part of the book (and in the book as a whole). Richard Allen discusses the idea that women's art which is radical is likely to be avant-garde, Dinah Birch considers how women writers have transgressed the conventions of genre, and Joan Swann asks whether women get more power by adopting forms of speech hitherto associated with men or by adopting their own 'female' forms.

Conventions have also controlled whose 'self' may be publicly exhibited and of interest in society; portraits in paint, in words, in marble show individuals who are famous or notorious, but fame or notoriety are regularly defined by conventions focused on public life. Women do fall within these definitions – though often because of some connection with a man, or as some kind of generalized being such as Britannia or Queen Victoria – but a survey of any town or gallery or shelf of biographies will show that it is men who are more often given this attention.

► **ACTIVITY 1** ◄

To get a glimpse of what it means to strike against this, stop here and read Evelyn Haythorne's autobiography, *On Earth to Make the Numbers Up*.

The first section of Book Four is, finally, crucially concerned with the process whereby representations are made by some and taken up by others, and how far this is a gendered process. As ever, meaning in this last sentence arises from the codes and messages in it and the context in which it appears. 'Representation', for example, comes from a more general code and one which avoids the questions about value that arise with the word 'art'. 'Representation' has also a nicely inclusive quality emphasizing that we see common processes in all forms of arts and crafts; women are represented in words and in paint and we read a picture just as much as we read a story. 'Representation' also avoids the idea that we can find simple reflections of reality in art or anything similar; some other process of coding has always intervened.

Using the word 'made' again provides a useful general term; often the word 'production' is used, as in Richard Allen's article, to carry the implication that the production of representations can be analysed in the same way as the production of washing machines or violins. Both terms avoid for the time being the problems that can arise in using the word 'creativity'. We are happy to say, with Dinah Birch, that Virginia Woolf was 'creative'; we would be less happy to say that a pornographer is in the same way 'creative' in his representations of women.

After reading this part of *Imagining Women*, we hope you will have a more self-consciously critical and enquiring attitude to questions about the making of representations based upon a clear conceptual framework. The key terms of that framework are introduced in the articles as follows:

Article 1.1: art, hierarchies of value, skill, binary concepts, shifting signifiers, creativity;

Article 1.2: discourse, genres, realism, power, ideology, the author and the reader;[1]

Article 1.3: genre, the right of entry to a cultural territory, psychoanalysis, romance;

Article 1.4: language, injunctions against speaking, speech as a form of social practice, interruptions.

Start by reading the introduction to Chapter 1 (pp. 13–14).

ARTICLE 1.1 'MAKING THINGS MEAN' BY CATHERINE KING

Please now read Article 1.1 (pp. 15–20).

► **ACTIVITY 2** ◄

As you read the article, make a note of your responses to the following questions:

(a) How does King define art?

(b) What positive step does her analysis of past art allow her to make?

COMMENT

King's aim is to define art in the broadest terms possible, stressing the potential openness of boundaries and pushing them out so as to include a range of things conventionally excluded, such as 'the shaping of the human body'. While study of art of the past may initially trap one within its conventions, further work shows that definitions of art have shifted a number of times in the past. Thus perhaps feminists are not aiming at a unique gesture of revaluation but are working with boundaries which have always been flexible.

[1]That key issues are dealt with here in the one article by a man is both odd and, hopefully constructively, provocative. It will be odd to you if you think that a man intrinsically cannot achieve that transgressive reading which may be necessary to overturn the almost compulsory mutually exclusive equations of men with the public, with buildings etc. and women with caring and the private to which Catherine King refers (Article 1.1, pp. 16–18), or to overturn the kind of patronizing attitude to women's work which Dinah Birch quotes (Article 1.3, pp. 48–9). It will be more positively provocative if it causes you to reflect further on the shifting nature of the subject, and to 'place' yourself and your own readings of the text offered in the book. Perhaps this will lead you to reflect not only on your own 'right of entry to ... cultural territory' (Birch, Article 1.3, p. 47), but also to the way that right is continually negotiated and renegotiated.

ACTIVITY 3

What does King see as forming what she calls women's 'art-making'? Briefly note down your answer.

COMMENT

King suggests that the following are important:
- Segregation of art forms based on gender and placing women's segregated forms as inferior.
- Men's control over women's involvement in art-making.
- The binary opposition of women/men as private/public and the higher valuing of the public.
- Definitions of skilled making which again segregate and value or devalue.
- Women's desire to redefine boundaries.

ACTIVITY 4

Make a note of your response to the following question:

What is the value of 'knowing something of the way the system works' (p. 19)?

in order to subvert the ideologies of the system.

COMMENT

We can use our understanding of how the process operates to see how it is characterized not by neutral definition but by attempts to exclude and control in a way which will remind you of segregations and discriminations in other areas of women's work. The underlying situation seems also to have a degree of permanence ('what they signify remains the same': p. 19). But, against that, King argues that what we see is the result of change in history; the process, however entrenched, 'can be shifted' (p. 19). Key to the shift is the change for women from being objects in men's definitions ('others') to their being able 'to define *our* diversities and *our* creativities' (p. 20). In thinking about 'binary concepts' we move also from thinking of 'either ... or' and from seeing differences as structuring hierarchy, since women's art-making is invariably on the down side in these ways of thinking, to thinking of 'and' and seeing differences between women's and men's art-making as structuring diversity (pp. 17–18).

SET BOOK: *WAYWARD GIRLS AND WICKED WOMEN*

▶ ACTIVITY 5 ◀

Please now read the introduction and the following stories from the set book.[2] These stories are used in Articles 1.2 and 2.2, but they may also help you think through the more conceptual articles in Chapter 1.

Elizabeth Jolley, 'The Last Crop'
Leonora Carrington, 'The Débutante'
Bessie Head, 'Life'
Suniti Namjoshi, 'Three Feminist Fables'
Angela Carter, 'The Loves of Lady Purple'
Jamaica Kincaid, 'Girl'

ARTICLE 1.2 'ANALYSING REPRESENTATIONS' BY RICHARD ALLEN

Please now read Richard Allen's article from the beginning on page 21 as far as the heading 'Systems of Representation' on page 26.

▶ ACTIVITY 6 ◀

Allen begins with examples of what it means to say that all images work within conventions. Test this idea out for yourself by repeating the analyses he describes with your own material.

(a) Look at the way an event is shown in a range of newspapers and on television, particularly if something happens while you are working on this material which achieves wide prominence, as the Gulf War did while Allen was writing.

(b) Look also at a photograph of yourself or perhaps one you took of someone else. It might be interesting to share this activity with another student to see how far your sense of the meaning of the images and the conventions involved coincide.

The painting by Manet, to which Allen refers in the second section of his article, is reproduced here as Figure 1, along with the 'against the grain' image *Blasphemy* by Jean Fraser in Figure 2.

[2]We hope, of course, that the taste the set reading gives of Carter's anthology will encourage you to read further, either now or later.

CHAPTER 1 THEMES AND ISSUES: GENDER, GENRE AND REPRESENTATION

Figure 1
Edouard Manet, *Le Déjeuner sur l'Herbe* (*The Picnic*), 1863, oil on canvas, 208 x 264 cm., Musée d'Orsay, Paris. Photo: Réunion des Musées Nationaux Documentation Photographique

Figure 2
Blasphemy. Photography by Jean Fraser from *Celestial Bodies*, in *Stolen Glances*, edited by Tessa Boffin and Jean Fraser, 1991

ACTIVITY 7

Analyse Fraser's photograph, identifying how it draws on conventions, such as those employed by Manet, and how it disturbs these.

COMMENT

Overall, the representation disturbs conventions. At the most basic level it copies a painting but by using photography – a medium which occupies a position on the boundary of 'art'. The subject matter is also transgressive. That said, Fraser's photograph does draw directly on Manet's painting. Fewer characters are included, but the three figures are posed in a very similar way to the three foreground figures in *Le Déjeuner*. The basket also echoes the shape in Manet's work. Independently or through Manet, the photograph also draws on one of the strongest conventions in western art – namely, that it is appropriate for figures to be depicted in relation to nature and natural things. Here, again as is conventional, that relationship is ideal and harmonious. There is no sign of a storm, and the naked figure appears to feel no cold, as the clothed figures feel no excess heat. This harmony between the individual and nature conventionally obscures the relations which exist between the individual and the landscape – the person depicted may own the place depicted, for example, or be a servant to someone who does.

The form and the structure of the image could be said to be conventional in suggesting the realistic, and it does not strike against convention by transposing the sexes, showing a naked man and clothed women, which would suggest that the representation was of masculine/feminine gender relations. Fraser's transposing of the men into nuns shows that the subject is the nature of femininity seen as distinct from and excluding masculinity. The context of the image – a book entitled *Stolen Glances: lesbians take photographs* (Fraser and Boffin, 1991) – also constructs this meaning. Beyond that, the image may be as ambiguous and provocative as that of Manet. Is the meaning you read that, within femininity, the categories 'naked' and 'clothed' have lost their attachment to power? Or is the meaning the reverse of this, that 'clothed' is as powerful a sign of sexuality as 'naked'? Is the representation most importantly concerned with the nakedness of the left-hand figure or the clothedness of the nuns?

A third meaning, again in the context of the book, might spring from the conscious artifice of this image which contrasts with the realism of many of the photographs by other women in the collection. All these figures, perhaps all lesbians, or even perhaps all women (the photograph is saying), play artificial roles.

Finally, it may be worth noting that this image adds to the context in which we see Manet's painting, contributing further to a context in which it is understood that all people define their genders and play parts almost independent of their sex. Here the men and women do not play conventional parts – although whether one could go further and retitle the picture *Gay Men and Lesbians on a Picnic* is a question here left open.

Now read from the beginning of the section entitled 'Systems of Representation' on page 26 to the end of the section entitled 'Creativity' on page 33.

▶ **ACTIVITY 8** ◀

Look again at Leonora Carrington's 'The Débutante' in *Wayward Girls and Wicked Women* and think about the following questions as you do so:

(a) In the light of what you have just read in Allen's third section 'Systems of Representation', what discourses is the story formed within?

(b) Is this a radical story in the context of Allen's section on the 'Degrees of Freedom'? Does it contain 'liberated knowledge' (p. 33)?

COMMENT

This is not only the shortest but one of the strangest stories in the collection. Leonora Carrington's story works within a realistic fictional discourse – the everyday life of the story teller is described – but within a discourse which one might see as relating to fairy stories or the fantastic. It is also within the 'I' autobiographical discourse. The whole situation of the hyena going to the ball – with the inference that those who like society balls are akin to hyenas – marks it as radical, and the horror that comes with the realistic details of the hyena eating the maid creates a very disturbing story. But overall it is difficult to decide whether this is 'liberated knowledge'. Does the ending suggest a representation of the mutual rejection of child and parent – the mother cries 'the thing that was in your place ... cried out; " ... I don't eat cakes!"' (*Wayward Girls and Wicked Women*, p. 24). Or is it telling the reader that the usual magical resolutions of fairy stories simply serve patriarchy (sadly men do not turn into princes) and that the ideology women should learn is altogether more threatening? Or is it all too horrifyingly fantastic to achieve any relation to the real world?

Now read to the end of the article (pp. 34–42).

▶ **ACTIVITY 9** ◀

Look again at the first five pages of Elizabeth Jolley's story 'The Last Crop' (pp. 1–5 in *Wayward Girls and Wicked Women*):

(a) How far can the opening of the story be said to show power relations?

(b) And how far do these pages seem to be 'established art' which Allen describes as involved in the 'authorizing of a particular partial truth as the sole truth in the interests of a particular class' (p. 37)?

COMMENT

The story begins with a representation of the power relations of school 'Home Science' and continues to focus on domestic work – one of the markers of women's inequality. But the sense that the 'I' represented is in a subservient position is countered by the way she is the story teller – and thus ostensibly in control of the representation. The ideological 'truth' that women have some special relation with housework is also undercut by the mother's commonsense notion that poor people can quite properly 'steal' some of those pleasures enjoyed by the rich. The opening of the story, then, depends upon the tension between these two ideologies – on the one hand that it is natural for the rich to have more and to have servants etc., and on the other that it is natural for other people to use things while the rich are away, that property is not sacred. The balance is tipped towards the second position for the reader because we have no direct access to the feelings of the rich in this story and live within the real world of the mother and child. That said, the fact that Jolley retains the rather puzzled child as the narrator keeps the reader in a state of similar puzzlement for the time being. It is not clear either whether power relations within the family have been disturbed here or whether there is orthodoxy. The innocent and undeveloped mind at the centre of events and of the narration represents the relation of the questioning, disrupting ideology to orthodoxy. It also plays a key part in establishing our sense that this story will ultimately be in the service of women, questioning the nature of what Foucault calls 'government' (in Article 1.2, p. 35).[3]

During the time that you are studying Chapter 1 of Book Four, you will have the chance to view Television Programme 07 entitled *Outside In: women artists and cultural difference*. It is important for you to view this broadcast in terms of the way it shows the concerns of those women representing (themselves) who are interpreted in a 'western' context and, often, conventions of meanings, but who wish to assert their non-western identities, as well as their rights to representation as women artists. In the programme, Rita Keegan, Zarina Bhimji and Mona Hatoum talk about how they, personally, inform their representations with their Dominican, Asian and Arabic identities and strategies for refusing western interpretations of their statements, as 'primitive', 'decorative', 'like Gauguin and Picasso'. Since in these weeks' work we are taking our overview of the systems which control the powers of representation, it is crucial to keep thinking about differences in different womens' cultural locations, with regard to imagining themselves and others.

---

[3] Article 6.2, 'Feminism, Criticism and Foucault' by Biddy Martin, in Book One, is also relevant to this topic.

CHAPTER 1 THEMES AND ISSUES: GENDER, GENRE AND REPRESENTATION

ARTICLE 1.3 'GENDER AND GENRE' BY DINAH BIRCH

Dinah Birch's article looks in more detail at the issue of genre raised by Richard Allen in the fourth section of the previous article; her aim is to track the relation of literary forms to external forces and then to extend the argument to consider 'internalized factors' that might explain why women write in one form rather than another.

> Please now read Article 1.3 from the beginning on page 43 to the line ' ... on the removal of those external factors as the way forward' (the end of the first paragraph on page 50).

► **ACTIVITY 10** ◄

What kind of programme might follow from a desire to concentrate on 'the removal of those external factors' in relation to poetry? Make a note of your response.

COMMENT

First, perhaps women would need to have more independence – in Virginia Woolf's phrase, women poets, like women Open University students, need 'a room of one's own'. Then, education needs to be available freely, and to women of different classes and different ethnic groups, so that women can gain automatic entry into that world dominated by the classics and the English pentameter – they need to be able to emulate Woolf again in being able to use established and orthodox language, to have command over the use of the patrician 'one' form of speech. Such an analysis may, however, seem only relevant to the past; with some hesitation Birch uses the words of Harold Bloom to project the argument into the future. In a world in which women's liberation has been achieved, the 'external factors' and the 'ancient rules' themselves will change – 'Homer will cease to be the inevitable precursor' (p. 49). The myths of orthodoxy themselves will be changed. So, on the one hand, the programme for women involves working to gain access to the institutions which allow men to write poetry and possess the most prestigious genre, and on the other, it involves working for change in gender-, class- and race-biased 'ancient rules' (p. 49), external factors which will inevitably lead to a change in the valuing of women's work.

In the second part of the article, where Birch deals with 'internalized factors', she raises issues also dealt with in Article 5.1, 'Lacan' by Rosalind Minsky, in Book One. Birch links the ideas more directly to language and literature, drawing on the work of Hélène Cixous. Finally, she discusses the genre of romance.

> Please now read from the paragraph beginning 'Few feminists would want to argue with that ...' (p. 50) to the end of the article on page 55.

ACTIVITY 11

Do either the ideas of Cixous, or the romance, offer the possibility of change and redefinition, analogous to that which might follow from external factors? Briefly note down your response to this question.

COMMENT

Cixous's emphasis on women's making being like 'the torment of getting up to speak' (p. 51) represents a difficulty every bit as great as that involved in overturning the external forces. Birch suggests that from this torment arises 'fragmentation, hysteria and madness' as signs of the difficulty of finding speech. In this she echoes the title of Gilbert and Gubar's classic work of feminist literary criticism *The Madwoman in the Attic* (1979) which in turn refers to Charlotte Brontë's *Jane Eyre*. The notion of a kind of madness in women's writing may also remind you again of 'The Débutante'. Does this represent, in Cixous's words (p. 51) someone 'lost for words, ground and language slipping away'? The answer could be 'yes', particularly if one picked out the controlled sentences: 'She had eaten all round the face very carefully so that only what she needed remained. "You've been really neat," I said' (*Wayward Girls and Wicked Women*, p. 24) and contrasted it with: 'A bat came in through the window uttering little cries. I am terribly frightened of bats. My teeth chatter, I hid behind a chair. Hardly was I on my knees before the beating of wings was drowned by a loud noise at my door' (ibid.). In these final sentences, language does seem to be slipping away, but if one takes a clue from the biographical note – 'she was a close associate of the Surrealists' (ibid., p. 336) – one can construct an alternative reading. This would emphasize not the loss of control and the slipping from a realistic discourse, but Carrington's use of a more dangerous and transgressive discourse whose function is to disturb. The discourse used in the story can also be seen to have a longer history if it is seen as part of the genre known as the Gothic[4] novel which arose in the late eighteenth century but was largely repressed by the firm realist forms of the nineteenth century. Ellen Moers in *Literary Women* writes: 'As early as the 1790s, Ann Radcliffe firmly set the Gothic in one of the ways it would go ever after: a novel in which the central figure is a young woman who is simultaneously persecuted victim and courageous heroine' (Moers, 1978, p. 91).

---

[4] Gothic novels are characterized by the use of dark and mysterious settings, mystery, horror and fear. Typically, in earlier examples such as Ann Radcliffe's *Mysteries of Udolpho*, a young woman may be found trapped inside a large elaborate and dark castle, pursued by violent and mysterious forces. Later and different examples of the genre include Mary Shelley's *Frankenstein*, and in many ways the works of Emily and Charlotte Brontë.

ARTICLE 1.4 'WAYS OF SPEAKING' BY JOAN SWANN

As you work on the final article in Chapter 1 – 'Ways of Speaking' by Joan Swann – try to set it beside the work you have just done on Dinah Birch's article. In the second section of her article Birch requires you to think within a context drawn from Lacan and psychoanalysis in thinking about women's poetry and the forms of writing. In contrast, Joan Swann puts a greater stress on social factors and draws on empirical research in her discussion of women's language. You will, no doubt, form your own view as to which, if either, of these two strategies you feel carries greater weight, but it is important to note that, as Book Four asks you to push at the boundaries of what is considered art, so it asks you – as is so often the case in women's studies – to push at the boundaries which define how one may think about a subject. It is as valid to think about representations in terms of psychoanalysis – apparently the preserve of medicine or psychology – and to explore large theoretical hypotheses about masculinity and femininity, as it is to think about them in terms of the analysis of everyday speech interaction and observations of the 'real' world.

Language studied directly offers an important and useful way of ending this chapter. Our reading of a 'work of art' is akin to a conversation in which we play the part of the listener, attentive to the words of the speaker. The external factors which barred women from poetry find an analogue in the 'institutional constraints that have acted as "regulatory mechanisms"' (p. 58), militating against women's participation in public forms of speaking. Such a view supports the notion of a divide, a binary opposition in which one is either man *or* woman, caught in the ideological imperatives of a particular class.

Please read Article 1.4 (pp. 56–66) now.

► **ACTIVITY 12** ◄

Make brief notes on your answer to the following question:
What does the section 'Women and Men Speaking' tell us about women and men as language groups?

COMMENT

Although only brief evidence from an ongoing debate is presented, it does seem arguable that women's speech can be distinguished from men's speech. The debate began with a linguist like Lakoff working in a tradition in which intuitions about how women and men spoke were advanced as evidence. It has developed, drawing increasingly on evidence of how women and men interact. This suggests that speech differences do seem to coincide with power relations, so that, for example, the power an individual has as a member of a social group is signalled by the ability to interrupt the speech of someone in another, inferior group. The process is a dynamic one; the information collected by observation urges us to see speakers as members of speech-groups but to see those groups as shifting, and to emphasize also the individual nature of speech and the importance of the particularity of context of each speech interaction – as Swann writes: 'all speakers have to balance different aspects of their identity – what is salient in one context may be played down in another' (p. 62).

► **ACTIVITY 13** ◄

As a final activity in this part of Book Four, try to relate the ideas in Joan Swann's article about the links between gender and power, with those in the other articles in Chapter 1.

COMMENT

Swann identifies power relations organized according to a hierarchy based on gender which can be detected in speech interactions, and also power relations operating in 'customs and practices that distribute speaking roles unequally between women and men' (p. 59). The power relations which can be found in everyday speech seem like the ripples from a stone thrown into a pool, to spread wider and wider into language interactions and the language of stories, poems and plays. They spread into other 'languages' in paintings, scripture, photographs and other 'art-makings', and beyond art into technology and the whole fabric of society.[5]

This generally expressed idea can be given a particular focus through the brief interaction quoted from West and Zimmerman. Catherine King begins her article wanting to 'stress the potential openness of art's boundaries and partitions' (Article 1.1, p. 15). Just the opposite of that is contained in the male's 'I've got everything jus' how I want it in that notebook (.) you'll screw it up leafin' through it like that' (p. 61). The female is here a disruptive force and disruption is negative and threatening; in just this way, established male-dominated conventions have everything in place and resist the 'leafin'

---

[5]Here, if you have time, look back to Article 1.2, 'Women's Voices/Men's Voices: Technology as Language' in Book Three, *Inventing Women*, where Margaret Lowe Benston writes: '... technology itself can be seen as a "language" for action and self-expression with consequent gender differences in ability to use this "language" ... men's control over technology and their adherence to a technological world view have consequences for language and verbal communication and create a situation where women are "silenced"' (Book Three, p. 33).

through it' that questions what appears naturally true. The sense of natural truth that accumulates round traditional views also conceals the fact that 'truth' acts in a particular interest – 'everything jus' how I want it'.

The male cutting into the female speech, and the female's consequently unfinished sentence, stand as a symbol of the alienation feminists interested in psychoanalysis find in the relation of women and language (see Article 1.3, p. 50). Finally, the analysis of power relations at this precise and particular level relates to the need 'ceaselessly to deconstruct' discourse and to understand, in Foucault's words, the 'finer, more detailed phenomena' which tell the truth (see Article 1.2, pp. 41, 35).

3
CHAPTER 2 LITERARY REPRESENTATIONS: SELF AS SUBJECT (WEEKS 26 AND 27)
(prepared by Lizbeth Goodman)

For the next two weeks, your main task will be to read Chapter 2 of *Imagining Women*. The title of this chapter, 'Literary Representations: Self as Subject', reflects the form to be studied as the major thematic concern of the articles included in this part of the course – literary representations: that is, writing, or written essays, documents and stories of various kinds. The common theme of this part of the book is the relationship of women's lives to their positions as authors, as women, as feminists and as active creators of images of women as characters.

You might find it helpful to divide these two weeks' work into two sets of tasks. For instance, the introduction to Chapter 2 and Articles 2.1 to 2.3, along with associated reading from the set book *Wayward Girls and Wicked Women*, could be covered in the first week (Week 26); and Articles 2.4 to 2.7, along with associated reading from the set book *On Earth to Make the Numbers Up*, could be covered in the second week (Week 27). While this plan will not suit everyone, it is offered as one workable and sensible way of handling this material.

If you divide your work in this way, you will find that the first week's readings focus on feminist criticism of literature and on literature by women: short stories and science fiction. The second week's work continues the study of fiction by women but shifts genres to poetry, and then shifts again to a very different kind of writing: literary criticism about autobiography, and working-class women's autobiography.

In reading and thinking about all of these different kinds of literary representations, you will encounter a number of themes and ideas. These can be thought of in terms of aims and objectives, or less formally as ways of approaching the readings which will help you to understand them and to see their relevance to the book and the course as a whole.

Key ideas and aims

It will be helpful, before you start the reading, to think through a few key ideas which you will encounter in the next few weeks. While the two weeks' work can be divided in half, as suggested above, there are broad themes and ideas which run right through this section on literary representations. You might find that they are best thought of as guiding ideas which – if kept in mind as a broad outline – may help to focus your reading.

The main ideas which arise in this two weeks' work are:

- The idea that there is a difference between writing as a woman and writing as a feminist (or reading as a woman and reading as a feminist).

- The idea that women are the writers of literature, as well as its subjects and readers. We can, therefore, practise reading with attention to women's roles as writers, as well as readers and interpreters of works of fiction.

- The distinction between fiction and non-fiction.

- The idea that different kinds of literature – from literary criticism to short stories, from poetry to autobiography – are similar in the sense that they are representational forms created through the use of words (written language) as a medium to create images and to convey ideas.

Most importantly for this course on issues in women's studies, it is important to think of this work on literature in terms of the larger issue of women's representation in, by and through language. Spoken language was addressed earlier, particularly in Article 1.4 by Joan Swann, but we can also think critically about writing as a means of representation of and by women.

Obviously, these objectives are closely related. Some of them may seem a bit lofty or abstract to you now, but as you read the articles in Chapter 2, these ideas should become clearer. It might therefore be helpful to come back to this 'checklist' after you have done the reading, in order to check that your understanding of the materials can be focused and associated with this checklist of key aims and ideas.

LITERARY REPRESENTATIONS: SELF AS SUBJECT

The first idea to wrestle with is the meaning of the title of this chapter. The many and varied forms of literary representations have already been introduced and will become familiar as you work your way through the chapter. But the relationship between literary representations – as one form of cultural representation which can be studied in relation to gender – and the concept of 'self as subject' is one which requires some explanation.

In all the readings and activities you will encounter in these two weeks, one major idea is repeated, though it appears in different ways in different contexts. This is the idea that self is subject: that the self (the individual's ways of thinking about herself, expressing herself, constructing her identity, representing herself and acting in society etc.) can be and often is the subject of women's fiction and literary representations of various kinds. Feminist criticism, for instance, studies writing by women: it takes women's literary self-representation as its subject. Fiction – prose and poetry – may be written by women and have women as the subjects: not only as heroines but also as active characters initiating change within their own stories.

In autobiography, women literally write about themselves. We cannot always interpret autobiographical writing as 'fact' rather than 'fiction' however. What is included and excluded from autobiographical accounts, and indeed what point of view the author takes, will influence the literary representation of self which she creates. All these different forms of literary representation can therefore be studied with regard to the relationship between the author's intentions and her position in relation to the text itself. Now let's get down to some reading, the basis of any study of literature, or of literary representations.

CHAPTER 2 INTRODUCTION

First of all, read the introduction to Chapter 2 (pp. 67–72).

The introduction to Chapter 2 raises a number of key issues or ideas which arise in this part of the book, all of which will help to focus your reading of the articles which follow. These ideas are:

1 The positions of writers are often expressed in their writing.

2 Our positions as readers are influential in the ways we read and in our interpretations of what we read.

3 Writing is an art form, or a form of creative expression (with words, or written language, as the medium) which can be used as a form of self-representation.

4 Women writers may write from very different positions (influenced by age, ethnicity, sexuality, physical ability, and experience of social marginalization, class etc.), and may write in different forms (fiction, including prose, poetry and drama, or non-fiction in the form of academic criticism, autobiography, biography, journalism etc.), and in any number of different styles (realistic, unrealistic, stream of consciousness, formal academic style etc.). All of these factors may influence the writing.

5   Social circumstances or context will also be likely to have some influence on the process of creative writing and on the production of literary representations of various kinds. Political contexts, for example, or cultural policies on censorship and publication, sexual political hierarchies in the publishing industry and political–legal factors such as, in the UK, the implementation of Section 28 (regulating the 'promotion of homosexuality') or the continuing influence of sexism and racism in society, will influence the degree to which any author will be free to express her politics, sexuality or personal vision within any given cultural context at any given time. And of course, the ways in which any writer's perspectives may have been influenced by social construction or larger psychological and social factors may also be analysed.

6   Our ways of engaging with what is written will tend to be influenced by similar factors.

This part of the book also deals with the idea (discussed at length in the book introduction) that women's personal experiences, roles and views of self may be portrayed in their writing, or may influence their writing in more subtle ways (for instance, through positioning the narrative voice in a work of fiction, or through the selection of information to be included in and excluded from biography and autobiography).

There is one last point to keep in mind: some women writers believe that there is a unique 'women's voice' which emerges from women's writing. Others do not. There is no right or wrong way of looking at this complex issue, and in the articles which follow, a variety of perspectives are put forward. Keep this issue in mind as you read.

ARTICLE 2.1 'THE FEMINIST CRITICAL REVOLUTION' BY ELAINE SHOWALTER

Please read Article 2.1 now (pp. 73–78).

Article 2.1 has been taken from the introduction to Elaine Showalter's book *The New Feminist Criticism* (Showalter, 1985), in which she describes the impact of feminist criticism on academia, literature and culture since the 1970s.

In the section of her introduction which you have just read, Showalter posits the crucial idea that since the 1970s, feminism and feminist ways of reading have changed the focus of literary criticism, with the result that gender has been established 'as a fundamental category of literary analysis' (p. 73). She analyses this shift of focus in terms of developmental phases:

- Phase one: feminist criticism began by analysing stereotyped images of women and misogynist ways of representing women: a process which led to a change of perspective in readers and critics, leading to:

- Phase two: '… the discovery that women writers had a literature of their own, whose historical and thematic coherence, as well as artistic importance, had been obscured by the patriarchal values that dominate our culture' (p. 74). This led to the rediscovery and re-reading of works by women: writing women into history, and searching for texts written by and about women, leading on to:

- Phase three: since the mid-1970s, there has been a recognition of the dual origins of feminist literary criticism which arose not only from the advances in thinking in the women's movement but also from the more limiting legacy of patriarchal forms of literary criticism, largely formed within academic institutions (which were, of course, themselves male-dominated areas of privilege). This phase was initiated partially by the influence of American and European (especially French) feminist thought on British ways of thinking.

This third phase has opened up a whole range of important theoretical questions for feminist criticism: what is (or is there) a feminist aesthetic or 'women's style'? Is there a separate lesbian aesthetic? In what ways can all the different feminisms and feminist theories work to inform women's writing in the UK, or elsewhere? Showalter's article is longer in its original form, but our extract ends on a brief summary of developments in and influences on feminist literary criticism since the 1970s.

► **ACTIVITY 14** ◄

Go back and read the last paragraph of Showalter's article (p. 78). Summarize her main point(s) in your own words.

COMMENT

The main point Showalter makes in this paragraph is that the three phases (listed above) influenced the development of feminist literary criticism through the 1970s and into the 1980s, with the result that traditional values have been overturned and it is now necessary to attempt to find a '... complete revolution in the understanding of our literary heritage'. This is a project in which many feminist literary critics are engaged today.

You should have noticed that Showalter's article was published in 1985. Feminist literary criticism has come further in recent years. But Showalter's article is still the best summary of the points you will need to understand for this part of the course. The theoretical questions it raises have not been 'solved'. There have been many new books and debates on subjects such as 'women's voices', 'feminist aesthetics', 'lesbian representations' and so on, and also on the question of the best way to ensure that women's literature will henceforward be included in the 'canon'. But these subjects must be addressed again and again in each political context and generation.

One major development in recent feminist writing has been a recognition of the important contributions made by women of colour. Just as it took time before the influence of the women's movement began to be seen in the valuing of women's writing, so it took time before feminists in the West recognized the distinctive voices of women of colour. The following extract from an essay by Pratibha Parmar relates one woman's experience of this realization:

Words are Weapons

For me as a Black woman it is vital that our histories and our struggles are documented. It is vital, too, that we become visible in ways we can control. Writing is one way of doing this, where we can create images of ourselves through our visions and imagination, as well as challenge existing stereotypes. We must speak through whatever means are available to us, or we will be condemned to silence, misrepresentation and invisibility.

(Parmar in Chester and Nielson, 1987, p. 153)

One other development which is suggested but not extensively discussed in Showalter's article is also important: feminist criticism of literature is not necessarily the same as criticism of women's literature, or women's criticism of literature. Not all women writers consider themselves feminist, or intend to write feminist fiction. Yet some literature written by women can be read or interpreted in feminist ways.

Making distinctions between women's literature and art, and feminist literature and art, is not always easy. There is no handbook which can be consulted, no checklist of 'things to look for in feminist fiction', for instance. This is partly because there are so many different definitions of feminism and partly because questions of aesthetics and artistic worth are not easily distinguished from questions of politics. Thus, a possible discrepancy between the author's intent and the reader's or critic's ways of reading any given literary piece has been the subject of much recent literary criticism.

If you review the introduction to Chapter 2, you will be reminded that: 'One aspect of "the feminist critical revolution" which informed and complicated the choice of readings in this chapter, and in the book as a whole, is the ambiguous distinction between "feminist literature" and "women's literature"' (p. 68). This point is worth reconsidering here, as it will be raised in different ways in your reading and the associated activities in this part of the Study Guide.

Throughout the course, you have been asked to read and think about various essays and papers written by (predominantly) women. Most of these have been written from (and all can be read from) a feminist perspective. In this part of the course, we are very self-consciously telling you who the authors are. We are also making pointed references to the feminist intent of some of these authors.

▶ **ACTIVITY 15** ◀

Make a list of aspects of Elizabeth Jolley's story 'The Last Crop' in *Wayward Girls and Wicked Women* which seem to you to make it a 'feminist story'. Do you think there is a strong case for calling 'The Last Crop' a feminist story? Or, do you think it is more accurate (or safer) to think of it as an example of women's writing or a story by a woman?

COMMENT

There are many different aspects of this story which you might have included in your list. Aspects which seem to make it a feminist story are the female narration and focus on primarily female characters; the emphasis on powerful female roles and on women thinking and acting in order to do well by themselves and their children. You might have thought of other points. Or, you might have thought that the mother in the story is 'bad': not a good role model and therefore not a proper feminist subject. Either response would be correct. What is interesting is not your final evaluation of this or any story as 'feminist' or 'not feminist', but rather your entrance into the critical process of evaluation. In doing this activity, you 'did' some feminist literary criticism. The same activity could be done with any story. You might find this a useful exercise to discuss in a tutorial, for it is likely that other students and your tutor may have different points listed, and perhaps different conclusions as to whether this or any other story is 'feminist'.

The process of reading and evaluating the 'feminist' value of stories or other art forms can be quite challenging. There are not really any right or wrong answers, though some answers will seem better supported and more reasonable than others. It is often but not always true that the author's intention makes a significant difference in determining the 'feminism' of a story. When you come to study Chapter 3, you will discover that the same problem of defining feminism also applies to the visual and tactile arts.

Feminist criticism is one form of literary representation in which it is possible to say that a given author's intent is feminist: otherwise, it would not be feminist criticism. This is not so simple an idea as it seems. For, just as there are many different feminisms, and many different ways of being feminist, so there are many different kinds of feminist criticism. Showalter's article will be a valuable source for contextualizing the next two articles on fiction as a form of literary representation. In reading these, it will be most important that you keep in mind the subtle distinctions between writing *about* women (writing in which women are the subjects), writing *by* women, and specifically feminist writing. Reading Showalter's article should have helped prepare you to make these kinds of distinctions.

We can now begin to apply some literary critical techniques to our reading of fiction. You should have read the relevant stories in *Wayward Girls and Wicked Women*: Angela Carter's 'The Loves of Lady Purple', Suniti Namjoshi's 'Three Feminist Fables', Elizabeth Jolley's 'The Last Crop', Jamaica Kincaid's 'Girl' and Bessie Head's 'Life'. The first three of these are discussed in Article 2.2 in Book Four; the other two will be discussed in this Study Guide.

▶ **ACTIVITY 16** ◀

Re-read Angela Carter's introduction to *Wayward Girls and Wicked Women*. Then, look to the end of the volume where some details about the lives of the contributing authors are printed. Write a few phrases to describe the background of each of the five authors listed above: Carter, Namjoshi, Jolley, Kincaid and Head.

COMMENT

If you look only at these five authors, you will notice that their backgrounds and life experiences are very different. It is interesting to think about the ways in which these women's different nationalities might have influenced their political perspectives and 'ways of seeing' the world, and their ways of representing their perspectives in their stories.

As you will have noticed, Carter is English, Namjoshi is Indian, living in Canada, and Jolley now lives in Australia, although she grew up in the English Midlands. Apart from the countries of their birth and residency, all three women have travelled and lived in other countries. Kincaid is an Antiguan living in New York, while Head is a South African resident in Botswana.

ARTICLE 2.2 'SUPPLY AND DEMAND: WOMEN'S SHORT STORIES' BY LIZBETH GOODMAN

You should now read Article 2.2 (pp. 79–93).

Article 2.2 focuses on the stories by Carter, Namjoshi and Jolley. It considers the stories in relation to the short story as a form, and to the idea that women's short stories are created by and in relation to some rule of supply and demand. Goodman argues that 'supply and demand' is a major theme of all three stories, and is also a rule of the market economy which can be usefully borrowed and applied to the situation of women in patriarchal societies. The same idea is expressed in different ways in the two stories not discussed in this article: Jamaica Kincaid's 'Girl' and Bessie Head's 'Life' which we will look at closely now.

In contrast to Jolley's story, Jamaica Kincaid's story 'Girl' is told in colloquial prose – influenced by the author's Antiguan background – in a first person stream of consciousness narrative. It is included in the anthology, in keeping with Carter's project of encouraging readers to engage with different perspectives and different points of view. The themes of the story include the inter-relationships between generations and between mothers and daughters; domestic responsibility; development and awareness of sexuality; expectations of and for the girl growing up into the role of womanhood which is in turn expected, if not demanded, of her.

Before moving on to discuss 'Girl' as a story, it may be helpful to indicate what is meant by the phrase (used in the preceding paragraph) 'first person stream of consciousness narrative'. The concept of 'stream of consciousness' is probably most familiar from films wherein the events seem to flow from one to another according to some internal logic rather than to some external 'plot' or outline. However, although the concept of 'first person voices' is often discussed, not everyone may be familiar with it. The 'first person voice' is distinguished from the 'third person voice' (there is no 'second person voice') in the following way: the first person is the term for the style of writing which casts the narrator as the speaker. It is subjective and personal. By contrast, the third person is the term used for the style of writing which casts the narrator as a third party to the events described, the narrator describes actions and events which – apparently – did not happen to her or him. When this narrator seems to know everything, we call this an 'omniscient narrator'. There are many more subtle distinctions which could be made.

'Girl' is a good example of a first person narrative, while 'The Last Crop' is told in a third person narrative voice. But it is important for you to note that the first person is a device adopted by many women writers. It can be used to create a sense of identification between the narrator and the events and images of the story. The same devices are used in poetry, much of which is written in a first person voice. But use of the first person does not necessarily imply that the narrative voice *is* the author's voice, or that the experiences described really happened to the author: this distinction between the narrator's and author's voices will be discussed at greater length in relation to poetry in your work for

Week 27. It is any author's prerogative to choose a narrative style and voice with which to express it. Often, the first and third person voices are mixed within any one story.

The story of 'Girl' consists of a list of warnings to a young woman, repeated by rote. The source of these warnings is not specified, but it becomes apparent from the content and form of address that these are general cultural expectations of how the 'girl' should act: expectations passed down from the elders. Here is an extract:

> ... this is how to sew on a button; this is how to make a buttonhole for the button you have just sewed on; this is how to hem a dress when you see the hem coming down and so to prevent yourself from looking like the slut I know you are so bent on becoming; this is how you iron your father's khaki shirt ...

(Wayward Girls and Wicked Women, p. 326)

Only in the phrase 'the slut I know you are so bent on becoming' does the voice of another distinct character become recognizable: the 'I' who 'knows' is the voice of the mother surfacing in the voice of the daughter. In the double mother–daughter voice, a value system emerges. The daughter repeats insults and threats, and in them can be heard the voice of the mother, who was once a daughter hearing the same words. This is the legacy of cultural expectation for women: a value system imposed upon young girls from one generation to the next.

The value system says that 'Girl' is bad, or potentially bad. Badness is linked to sexuality: sex is dirty; the girl is dirty. At no point within the narrative is the value system itself questioned; at least, not directly. The questioning of values is indirect: it emerges in the complicated element of self-recrimination which creeps into Girl's voice as she externalizes the words which are her internalized values. Identification of the source of guilt and unease in Girl's voice and reassessment of the values which inform the story are interpretive tasks assigned to the reader (assigned by Kincaid – the author – in her style). But Carter also sets an agenda for the reader of this story, contained in her introductory remark about the 'hypocrisy' of the sexual double standard.

Bessie Head's story 'Life' also deals with the issue of sexual blaming. In Head's story, however, there is more of a suggestion that the blame is 'justified', at least if cultural norms and values are kept in mind. The story trades in the themes of sexuality and desire, blame, violence, social relations and expectations for the behaviour of 'the good wife'. The word 'trades' is carefully chosen, for 'Life' is a story about supply and demand; about prostitution as men's demand and women's supply – a 'trade' in which men as 'clients' buy (or rent) women's bodies for sexual service, and also buy (or rent, or invent) images of women's bodies and women's roles in society at large. The story presents a community, or small society, which blames and punishes the supplier rather than the consumer, the prostitute rather than her client, the woman rather than the man. Carter's reasons for including this story in her anthology seem to be similar to the choice of 'Girl'. The echoes of *Fatal Attraction* are persistent.

The style of 'Life' is narrative prose, written in the third person as if the narrator were an 'objective' viewer of the events, or the 'fly on the wall' in a documentary. This is particularly significant given that the author herself (1937–1986) was a South African who moved to Botswana and did not live to see even the beginning of the breaking down of apartheid. 'When two worlds collide' is the keynote of the story. The two worlds are town and country (or more accurately, town and village). The protagonist is a young girl named Life, who returns to her native village years after her family left. She has been supporting herself as a prostitute, and soon has a flourishing trade in the village. The tension comes from the villagers' conflicting desires: to embrace Life as a native child, or to shun her as an immoral outsider. The tension mounts over the issue of Life's prostitution and the question of its valuation. The villagers must choose between viewing Life as an individual, or as a

Figure 3
James Caan and Kathy Bates in *Misery*, 1990.
Photograph: John Kobal Collection

Figure 4
Glenn Close, Michael Douglas and Anne Archer in *Fatal Attraction*, 1987.
Photograph: John Kobal Collection

representative of a way of life which their patriarchal society has an interest in protecting yet publicly condemning.

As Carter notes, Life is:

> ... thought to be bad, even wicked, not because she distributes her sexual favours but because she charges money for them, and, by doing so, disrupts the easy-going harmony of her village and transforms its most intimate relations into cash transactions. She imports the twentieth century into the timeless African village and is made to suffer for it, by a man who thinks he has the right to do so because he loves her.
>
> (Wayward Girls and Wicked Women, *p. xi*)

Figure 5
Meryl Streep, Roseanne Barr and Ed Begley Jnr in *The She-Devil*, 1989.
Photograph: John Kobal Collection

Life is killed by her husband in a jealous rage: a husband who is a known womanizer, but who cannot tolerate 'manizing' from his wife. Thus the double standard in this story ends in the death of Life, paralleled in the end of prostitution in the village (symbolizing the end of the market economy, when it benefits the woman more than the man). But of course, the market will reopen with new 'wares' soon enough. The husband is sent to jail, but given a relatively lenient sentence because as the (male) judge decrees, 'this is a crime of passion ... so there are extenuating circumstances' (*Wayward Girls and Wicked Women*, p. 44). These are the last lines of the story:

> A song by Jim Reeves was very popular at that time: *That's What Happens When Two Worlds Collide*. When they were drunk, the beer-brewing women used to sing it and start weeping. Maybe they had the last word on the whole affair.
>
> (*Ibid.*)

The worlds which collide in the story of 'Life' are not just town and country, but also female and male, outside and inside, subject and object.

Now that you have had a chance to consider each of these five stories separately, it will be useful to take a few minutes to look at them together, in relation to the idea of 'supply and demand'. In doing the following activity, you may find it helpful to look back at the first few pages of Article 2.2 where the idea of 'supply and demand' is discussed in relation to short stories in two ways: as a shorthand term for the dynamic of market forces which affects the politics of book/story production; and as a metaphor for the role and status of women – in different cultures – when a gendered double standard is in place.

ACTIVITY 17

Make a list of the kinds of books you might expect to find in an airport or supermarket sale bin, and a separate list of the kinds of books you might expect to find on the display cases and shelves of a book shop. Now break down that second list into the kinds of books you might expect to find in a popular high street book shop such as W.H. Smith's, in a general stock book shop such as Waterstone's, in an academic book shop such as Heffer's or Blackwell's, or in a specialist feminist book shop such as Sisterwrite or Silver Moon. Finally, ask yourself whether any of these lists (representing specific 'markets' for books) would be more likely than the others to stock short stories, or collections of short stories (as opposed to novels or non-fiction books).

COMMENT

You may have come up with lists something like these:

Bulk sale bins	**Book shop**
paperbacks:	*hardback and paperback books:*
spy/detective novels; thrillers; best-selling fiction; Mills and Boon romances; travel books; cookery books	textbooks and scholarly monographs (non-fiction); hardback and paperback fiction (including bestsellers and award-winning fiction, as well as 'the classics')

Bulk sale bins: as above

W.H. Smith: various kinds of popular fiction (as above) plus periodicals, children's books, maps etc.

Waterstone's: a wider selection of non-fiction and 'highbrow' fiction plus some selected (popular) non-fiction.

Heffer's: a selected range of popular and contemporary fiction, plus more academic textbooks and 'classic' literature, including literatures in non-English languages, plays and poetry as well as fiction, HMSO etc.

Sisterwrite: books by women, some fiction and some non-fiction, many of which will not be widely available at any of the above locations; also some art work by women, and some non-sexist children's books.

What is immediately evident is the large supply of pulp novels in airports and supermarkets compared with the relatively small supply of 'highbrow' short stories by women (for instance, *The Collected Shorter Fiction of Virginia Woolf* would not be likely to be found in a sale bin at the supermarket, while the latest Mills and Boon stories might well be found there). This situation is only significant if it is considered in the context of a publishing and sales industry which is largely male-controlled.

But the idea of 'supply and demand' is also used by Goodman as a metaphor for the role and status of women in relation to a gendered double standard. In this context, the phrase 'gendered double standard' is used to refer to the situation wherein women are treated or represented differently than men due to a set of expectations imposed by a male-dominated society. For example, if women are punished for adultery and promiscuity but men are not (as in Bessie Head's story 'Life'), the same standards are applied in two different ways, according to the gender of the person in question and the associated expectations of any given society in relation to culturally defined gender roles.

Of course, patriarchal cultures tend to have cultural gender roles which weigh to the side of men in the case of a double standard. This is the point which Head makes in her story of Life, and she does so by highlighting the idea that sex (prostitution) is profitable because it is in demand by men. Similarly, certain simplistic and stereotypical images of women – as angels and whores, for instance – are often depicted in literary representations by men. When women choose to depict similar characters, they may do so for subversive reasons: in order to explode those stereotypes, as in the five short stories discussed.

Goodman argues that 'supply and demand' is a metaphor which is appropriate to discussion of the short story as form, and of the representation of individual female characters within many women's short stories. You may have thought of other examples, perhaps from other stories, or from your own life experiences. This is fine: the important thing is that you understand the key points of the article, which are:

1. Literary representations of various kinds are produced and sold in the cultural market place, and must therefore be considered in a cultural context.

2. The short story is only one form of literary representation: one which has the advantage of being short and therefore not too demanding to read in terms of time, and which may therefore be suited to many women's busy daily lives.

3. The short story as a form is not limited by its length in its potential to be written from or interpreted in accordance with a feminist perspective.

4. The politics – or feminism – of the editor of an anthology are not necessarily reflected in the politics – or feminism – of all the authors included in that anthology (though it is fairly safe to call all the stories in *Wayward Girls and Wicked Women* 'feminist' to some extent, or at least to say that none is specifically anti-feminist).

Two more important ideas emerge from an analysis of Goodman's article in the context of the issues raised in Showalter's writing about feminist literary criticism: first, that the form of a literary representation (novel, short story, poem, autobiographical writing etc.) is related to and may influence its content; and second, that creating and interpreting literary representations are effective ways in which women imagine and re-present images of themselves. At times, the creation of literary representations may be an important way in which women – and particularly feminist – authors may begin to outline their most visionary images of self in society, perhaps sketching possible new societies and new ways of living as women in society, in the process.

Some of these same ideas are discussed by the three feminist authors featured in Radio Programme 08 *Writing From the Margins*.

▶ **ACTIVITY 18** ◀

Stop and review any notes you might have made on Radio Programme 08.

COMMENT

In Radio Programme 08, Susan Bassnett argued that while it is true that women's work in literature and most fields has been marginalized, it may also be true – at least for some authors – that the margins can be reclaimed in a subversive strategy of finding power where we are meant to be powerless. In this way, we can, when necessary, use our marginalization as a powerful position from which to work. Bassnett referred to the potential power of writing from the margins and 'sniping at the middle'. By this, of course, she does not imply that the marginalization of women's work is a good thing, but rather that we can, as feminists, find power in negative positions, and use that power to change things.

But Bassnett is not the only writer featured on that programme to interpret women's marginalization in potentially positive ways. Poet Alison Fell discussed her frustration at the lack of words to describe women's most emotional experiences, and explained that she finds it most useful to approach this as a challenge (rather than a stumbling block) in her writing. She creates new words, like 'grabbiting' and 'ragbitter'. Sara Maitland, a feminist novelist, similarly argued that the English language does not include enough words for the expression of women's experiences. She gives childbirth and the eroticism of the mother–child relationship as examples of experiences unique to women, which are difficult to describe with the words available in the English language. She further argues that the English language does not include positive words or phrases to describe the heterosexual sex act from the woman's point of view; she asks for a positive word or phrase to describe 'being penetrated', for instance.

If the margins are a powerful position from which to write – as these three authors, in different ways, all suggest – then what is the position of feminist science fiction writers? Suzette Haden Elgin is also referred to on Radio 08. She is a feminist science fiction writer and also a linguist and creator of the women's language Láadan. But not all writers of feminist science fiction are so expert at making up their own words. Some must try to use the words we have in existing languages. With this in mind, and remembering that science fiction tends to offer images of possible (usually future) worlds, what is the position of the writer of feminist science fiction? Is her place necessarily on the margins, and if so, is that necessarily a powerful position from which to write? Keep this question in mind as you read Frances Bonner's article next.

ARTICLE 2.3 'TOWARDS A BETTER WAY OF BEING: FEMINIST SCIENCE FICTION' BY FRANCES BONNER

Please now read Article 2.3 (pp. 94–102).

Frances Bonner's article describes some feminist science fiction stories and discusses them in detail. Here, it is important to note some more general points about feminist fiction in general, and feminist science fiction in particular.

Bonner points out that science fiction as a genre is most often associated with the genres of horror and fantasy. All three genres may include 'nova' such as BEMs (bug-eyed monsters). Yet, as Bonner points out, most feminist SF does not include BEMs or other creatures. The expectation that SF is likely to include such creatures may contribute to the marginalization of the genre, due to the prevalent social distaste for imaginary (slimy) creatures which are 'unrealistic', and viewed as childish and trivial. If SF is assumed to deal with subjects (and creatures) which are detached from reality, and therefore not 'important', the genre itself may also be seen as unimportant. Thus, incorrect assumptions about what SF is about may contribute to its marginalized status as a genre.

But if writing from the margins can be a powerful position, then perhaps writing about the margins – or about worlds which are so distanced from the present known world to be fantastic or unreal – can also be a powerful position. This is the position from and about which feminist science fiction writers write. And as Bonner concludes, the genre is a valuable political form which can be used in exploration of the implications of feminist arguments, even if the genre itself is 'sadly marginal' (p. 102).

> **ACTIVITY 19** ◀
>
> Go back and look at Activity 17 on booksellers. Is feminist science fiction mentioned in any of the listings? For that matter, is science fiction, horror or fantasy (feminist or not) mentioned? If feminist science fiction were to be included in one of the listings, which would it fit best?

COMMENT

Feminist science fiction is not listed; nor are science fiction, horror and fantasy. The fact that such genres are not included – and that most of you most probably did not miss them in the listings – says something about the cultural valuing of these forms of literature. Yet we might include science fiction, horror and fantasy literature with spy/detective novels and thrillers in the 'bulk sale bin' list. But perhaps not: the genres are quite different and do not necessarily share readerships. And where, if anywhere, would we place feminist science fiction? It would most likely be sold primarily, if not exclusively, at specialist feminist booksellers such as Sisterwrite.

There could be exceptions: some of Ursula le Guin's work, for instance, has reached a mainstream audience and might therefore be sold in highstreet bookshops as well. But the 'feminist' label is not easily applied to le Guin's more popular novels. A different exception to the rule might be Mary Shelley's *Frankenstein* which, as Bonner notes, can be seen as 'feminist science fiction' if the label is applied anachronistically. Frankenstein has achieved not only a cult status, but also an academic status and place on many English department course reading lists. Similarly, classic works which we might now call 'feminist science fiction', such as Charlotte Perkins Gilman's *Herland*, might be sold by academic and popular booksellers. But then this demonstrates 'supply and demand' in another sense: if books are included in the revised literary canon by their inclusion on university course reading lists, then booksellers are likely to stock them, not for ideological reasons but because books which are listed as 'suggested reading' are likely to sell. Contemporary authors have also reached mainstream audiences with what might be called 'feminist science fiction': Margaret Atwood's *The Handmaid's Tale* is an obvious example.

> **ACTIVITY 20** ◀
>
> Those of you who have access to local libraries might do an additional exercise. Go in and do a quick check to see whether any feminist science fiction titles are held there. You might do this most easily by using Bonner's bibliography as a checklist of titles to look for. If you cannot find them, you might ask the librarian why there is not a separate section on feminist science fiction (even if there is a section on science fiction). The answers you are likely to receive might be informative.

Perhaps the most important point raised in Bonner's article is the idea that the creation in feminist science fiction of all-female societies has specific social and literary functions; that is, these all-female societies are spaces (or worlds) in which the traditional cultural emphasis on the male, or on patriarchal assumptions, must be minimized and reviewed. Here, you may recall that Showalter stressed a change of focus from male to female perspectives as one of the major developments of feminist literary criticism.

In this regard, it is interesting to note that of all the diverse stories included in *Wayward Girls and Wicked Women*, none are examples of the SF genre. Carter's and Namjoshi's stories are the least realistic; they are like SF in some senses, but both rely on more acceptable forms: grotesque allegory and revisions of fairy tales. Carter's and Namjoshi's stories do exciting things within 'known' worlds. By contrast, feminist science fiction creates worlds of its own. With those worlds come new possibilities, but also new problems.

► **ACTIVITY 21** ◄

Make a list of some of the potential problems which might arise in a feminist SF world where there are no men.

COMMENT

You might have come up with any number of problems, large and small. Or, you might think that such a world would be ideal: no problems at all. The most obvious problem which might arise is related to reproductive technologies, though it is now possible to develop 'test tube babies' and the possibilities for all-female societies are becoming greater all the time. The question of biological determinism, however, still enters in. Who would be mothers and who would be 'fathers' (or would there be fathers at all)? Would all-female societies necessarily work according to clan systems, like some of the matriarchal Native American Indian societies, for instance? When one source of power and privilege is removed (in this case men/patriarchal power), does another take over? These huge questions are, in fact, the topics explored in some feminist science fiction. Other feminist SF, however, creates images of more harmonious worlds where power and privilege are not so problematic. Which seems more 'realistic' to you?

Bonner suggests that dystopias are often perceived as more credible than utopias. Perhaps we are all used to making the best of things in the world we know. It is harder to think of completely new worlds where common problems might not exist. Some argue that priority must be given to changing things in the world in which we live. This viewpoint may help to account for the relatively marginalized status of feminist science fiction, for it suggests that feminine action may be diffused if too many of us start writing (and reading?) science fiction. But others argue that the difficulty of planning and working in the 'real world' need not close off possibilities for other, better worlds; that indeed, it may be useful to imagine better worlds in order to work towards them.

SUMMARY

You have now read roughly half of the material on literary representations. The material covered so far has focused on feminist criticism of women's writing, and on fiction written by women (short stories and science fiction; as there was not time to ask you to read a full-length novel). In the three readings by Showalter, Goodman and Bonner, the focus is very clearly on feminist writing, rather than on women's writing in a more general sense. Goodman's article problematizes the issue of feminist authorship by pointing to the difference between the stated feminist intentions of an anthology's editor, and the (usually unstated) intentions of the authors of individual short stories. The important thing to remember is that each author writes from her own position, influenced not only by gender but also by race, class, age, sexual identity and any number of other factors.

In poetry, to a greater extent than in novels and short stories, the author's voice tends to be immediate, apparently in the first person. In some women's poetry, the subject matter is also very personal: for instance, in poetry about such themes as motherhood, sex, childhood experiences and so on. The next two readings in *Imagining Women* are written by poets, about the process of writing poetry. If you have time, you might do the following short activity, which has been designed to give you a head start on next week's work.

▶ ACTIVITY 22 ◀

Read the introduction to the Poetry Supplement and skim through the poems (but do not take more than half an hour over them at this point), considering the relationship between the themes outlined in the introduction.

COMMENT

The Poetry Supplement is organized by theme, and you will be doing some work later which will involve reorganizing some of the poems according to different themes. This thematic approach is the major way in which poetry is discussed in this course, though there are many other interesting ways to deal with poetry: stylistically, in terms of standard structures and rhythms, rhyme, alliteration etc. As this is an interdisciplinary course rather than a literature course, it is most useful and relevant to discuss poetry in terms of its implications for gender and writing (as a form of literary representation) rather than as a literary form *per se*. The two short readings on poetry by Ostriker and Rumens were included in Book Four for this reason: they describe, in the authors' own words, the process of writing poetry as one which involves making personal decisions and which is relevant to many aspects of their lives as women.

ARTICLE 2.4 'A WILD SURMISE: MOTHERHOOD AND POETRY' BY ALICIA OSTRIKER, AND ARTICLE 2.5 'MOMENT OF FAITH: WORKSHEETS' BY CAROL RUMENS

Please now read Articles 2.4 and 2.5 (pp. 103–107 and 108–112).

The most prevalent theme in both of these readings is that of motherhood as it relates to the writing of poetry. Both authors describe the process of giving birth as comparable in some respects to the act of creating a poem. While few feminists would argue that giving birth, or mothering, is not an important or significant activity, many would – and have – argued that the comparison of women's writing to childbirth is potentially dangerous, in several respects. In many western societies, for instance, mothering – and even the act of childbirth itself – is undervalued, seen as a 'women's activity' which need not be accorded too much cultural status, whereas tremendous cultural importance is often attached to fathering, from the heterosexual 'sex act' itself to the veneration of the father in patriarchies, and the attachment of symbolic significance to father figures in politics, history, literature and social life. Therefore, comparing women's writing to childbirth invokes the operative gender-based double standards which skew the valuing of women's creativity in all areas. Comparison of women's creative work in the arts and in literature to the more 'feminine' or 'domestic' or 'natural' role of motherhood may be dangerous in that it also invokes the dichotomy between private and public which is so often used against women. It has often been argued – particularly in Victorian times, but even today – that women's place is in the home, and that if women are to write at all, they may do so rather than have children, or they may write for children, or perhaps about children and other 'domestic' concerns (cookery, housewifery, romance etc.).

Of course, contemporary literatures by women have gone far beyond the limitations of such a view. But there are still good reasons for separating the personal from the public in the study of women's writing. What is raised in the Ostriker and Rumens articles is the question of the author's relationship to the image of self, or the voice, which emerges in her writing. The theme – motherhood and poetry – obviously raises this question in a rather more personal way than would, for instance, the same authors' treatments of a theme such as global politics or the economy. (Though that is not to say that there cannot be 'personal' poems about politics, or political poems about the personal.) What is at stake here is the relationship between the poet's voice and that which is heard in – or expressed through – her poems. Locating the author's voice is both less and more problematic in poets' articles about the process of writing poetry. For instance, in the articles by Ostriker and Rumens, the voice of the poet is easy to locate in one sense: the articles are written in the first person; the narrative voice is the poet's. But it is difficult to ascertain whether this voice is truly representative of the poet. Perhaps it expresses one mood, one idea, one way of working. Perhaps the poet has many different moods and voices: some of which are expressed in her poetry and some in her prose.

The work of several black women poets has also been included in this course. It is interesting to compare the treatment of the personal in the work of, for example, Grace Nichols and Jackie Kay with that of Ostriker and Rumens.

Read the article on Grace Nichols and her poetry, reproduced below, which appeared in *The Guardian* on 16 October 1991.

'If you ask me why I write, I will have to say I write for myself first, to have control, to make a world a little more to my liking' – poet Grace Nichols

FREE VERSE

Grace Nichols is constantly asked why she doesn't write more about the "realities" of being black. "As if there is only one reality. As if I am more a black than I am a woman, or a mother, or a poet." She kicks against this separating out of bits of her identity. "I refuse to be controlled in this way. I am all those things and no one thing." She calls herself proudly a "Caribbean person" with all that entails. "The mixture of races and cultures, American-Indian, Asian, European, African. If you are Caribbean, you are a citizen of the world."

The historical past used to make her angry; "But I've transcended that now, I know my own worth." Her native Creole language developed from plantation slaves yoking West Indian rap rhythm to borrowed English words. "Of course it was considered an inferior language, but I love it. And I use it not simply to preserve it, but because it is vibrant, exciting and alive."

The problem, she says, is "when it comes to black women, what people want is always their story. Never the black woman." And the story has to be one of hardship and struggle. She resents this: "Is this my purpose, the realities of black women? Do I have to be limited in this way?" We all have an interior life much more complex than the external realities. "I have to feel free to write about whatever I want. The poet I am is the woman in me, with all her possibilities, trying to have her voice heard. Tell them that I'll write a poem about my crotch if I please. That I'll make it light. Black writers are so bogged down in their past."

She wrote the poem about black realities anyway. "Maybe this poem is to say/that I like to see/we black women/full-of-weselves walking/crushing out ... the twisted self negating/history/we've inherited/crushing out/with each dancing step."

The main issue for Nichols, she says, has less to do with her race than with her gender. "To be able to write, to consider yourself a writer, you have to take yourself seriously. A man assumes that he is enitled to the time and attention he gets in his work, he extends a certain freedom to himself."

A male friend of hers, a poet, writing about deep-sea diving, recently took himself off on an exploration of the ocean bed for a month or so. "You don't find many women doing that." A woman has to find or steal her space. The imagination may know no boundaries but the domestic situation does.

Nichols is a mother of two daughters, Lesley, 18, from a brief marriage, and Kalera, two, the daughter of the poet John Agard with whom Nichols left her birthplace, Guyana, 15 years ago. The vast gap between her children was determined by her desire to write. "It was the only way I could find." But even now she admits that because of her work, her relationship with her elder daughter suffered. "We weren't always so close. I don't think I spent as much time with her as I should and I regret that. Maybe it's never good enough but I should have found a way of reassuring her."

She had thought she would have no more children but "John wanted a child" and five years ago, when she was eight months pregnant, she lost a son. "After that I said never again. I had to go through so much pain, it was exhausting and terrifying. You feel so alone and, in spite of the people around you, you know you are alone. Childbirth and death are so closely related but people don't acknowledge that."

Poetry, Nichols believes, comes from "a sense of loss", not from exaltation nor deep sadness. "It was the only thing that could fulfil that need in me, the wanting. The sense that when I left Guyana, I left so much behind. The culture, the people, feelings that can't be expressed in any other way than through poetry."

In poetry you are always trying to say the unsayable. "To touch people at a deeper level than mere words." It is hard to write poetry, "much harder than fiction". And it was only when she came to Britain that she became a "serious" poet. Here, where she saw black people "wrapped up in their coats of silence", she was forced to find an image of herself to reflect back. It is partly the perspective of the exile, the sense of being an outsider looking in. "It gives you a voice."

What mattered to her as a child, she says, growing up in Guyana, was that "you have no reflection of yourself in books". Her education was exclusively English and white. Black Beauty, Enid Blyton, Chaucer and Shakespeare. Her small niece, asked at school to write a piece about her family, described her mother, with fairy-tale blonde hair. Why did you do that, the women asked. "But we all knew the answer. Black women do not figure in literature, in stories."

To tell the truth of a powerful black mother at home would be to disfigure literature, to distort the myth. "It is schizophrenic for the child. You have your own rich black culture which you love. And you have the white hierarchy. You function between these two. Even now, people in the Caribbean still look to Europe, to America, as though they have everything. We have nothing. Theirs are the values to which we aspire. It's as though their own background isn't real, is inferior, secondary stuff. To make it big, you have to go outside."

It is the same, she says, with the white woman myth. "We all know the historical background, that during slavery a black man was lynched for even looking at a white woman." So the image grew of the white woman as unattainable and therefore desirable, "the white woman on a pedestal" above the black woman, while the black woman was appropriated by her white master. It effectively castrated the black man, says Nichols, but what did it do to the black woman?

"Black women are not so insecure about their sexuality," says Nichols. Not as insecure as the portrayal in Spike Lee's new film, Jungle Fever, in which a group of black women sit around talking about the white women who poach their black men. It is the black male, Nichols suggests, who is insecure, who looks to his past for excuses. Who conforms to the white stereotype. "The shiftless black Caribbean male," says Nichols and laughs. "You know there's a bit of truth in every stereotype. The men say it is part of their history, the result of slavery where the man didn't have control over his own offspring, where the children could be taken off and sold. And that's been handed down." But the women, as she says, did take responsibility. "They do not blame history."

Nichols came to England from Guyana when she was 27, when her own cultural identity was already intact, with few misgivings about who she was. She came partly because of practical reasons – the economic devastation of her country after independence in 1966 and the fact that there was not, and still is not, a Guyanese publishing house to support native writers. And partly through a rootlessness, a shiftlessness which is quintessentially Caribbean. A people dragged from one continent, Africa, to another, America.

Her mother, Iris, an intelligent woman, a lover of music, a talented pianist, had died from a stroke, prematurely, in her early fifties. A loving, tender woman whose life, Nichols says, was "circumscribed" by her seven children and her domineering husband. The day after her mother's burial, Nichols' father also dropped dead. He died, she says, of "no will to live". When she left she was not running away; there was nothing to stay for.

And her first cycle of poems, i is a long memoried woman, for which she won the Commonwealth Prize in 1983, celebrated her decision. It gave voice to the unheard, it sang the triumph of the disenfranchised slave girl. It looked back to myth and legend, to the spirits of centuries of silent black people, and it looked forward to a new birth, or rebirth. These poems did not eschew violence, nor quake with self-pity. Her bold use of "i" was her answer to what she calls "the twisted self negating history". Freedom became not just physical but moral, the search for a larger freedom: "I have crossed an ocean/I have lost my tongue/from the root of the old/one/a new one has sprung." Escape for body and soul, as in the tradition of all slave narratives, became one.

She has written two more volumes of poetry – Fat Black Woman's Poems and Lazy Thoughts of a Lazy Woman – completed one autobiographical novel and edited an anthology of black verse, Can I Buy A Slice of Sky. She is currently working on a new novel.

Figure 6
Grace Nichols. Photograph: *The Guardian*/Graham Turner

"If you ask me why I write, I will have to say that I write for myself first, to have control, to make a world a little more to my liking. Then, I suppose, for other women, black and white. But I can't compartmentalise myself. I don't like questions and I don't have answers. If I had the answers I probably wouldn't write at all."

(*Suzie Mackenzie, 'Public Lives' series in 'Women' section,* The Guardian, *16 October 1991, p. 37*)

► ACTIVITY 23 ◄

Now listen to one of the poems by Grace Nichols included on Audio-cassette 2, Side 1: 'The Fat Black Woman Goes Shopping'. In both *The Guardian* article and the poem, what visual image of the black woman is depicted? Does the image of the 'fat black woman' offered in the poem correspond with the image of Grace Nichols in the photograph which accompanies *The Guardian* article? Is either image necessarily the same as Nichols' view of herself? How can we know? Does the information which Nichols conveys in *The Guardian* article tell us enough about her to answer these questions? Make a note of your responses.

COMMENT

Your individual 'way of seeing' the 'fat black woman' of the poem will, of course, be influenced by your own position: by factors such as your own ethnicity, weight and body size, age, class and area of residence (whether you are, or know any fat black women). What is 'fat' but a relative term, like 'thin'? Your mental image of the fat black woman will be guided by the textual clue provided in the last line of the poem: 'nothing much beyond size 14'. The woman wears a size 14 or above. Or does she? Is Nichols the fat black woman? She does not look 'fat' to me. Does she see herself as fat? Or is the image of the poet separable and indeed separate from the image of the woman in the poem?

These are rhetorical questions: there are no right or wrong answers. Nichols created 'the fat black woman' and we each recreate her in our own mind's eye as we read the poem. Seeing the photograph of Nichols may have influenced our mental images of the woman in the poem. Reading Nichols' views on the multiplicity of roles and identities she is expected to reflect may also have influenced our images. The poem stands on its own, but is informed and enriched by a knowledge of the background and perspective of the poet. The same can be said of the work of Jackie Kay.

► **ACTIVITY 24** ◄

Now listen again to Audio-cassette 2, Side 1. In listening to Jackie Kay reading 'Mother Poem 2', 'So you think I'm a Mule?', 'Black Bottom', and 'Angela Davis', ask yourself whether you can identify any of the voices emerging from these poems with Jackie Kay's voice, and if so, which ones?

COMMENT

In the poems 'Angela Davis' and 'Black Bottom', the poet's voice (Jackie Kay's) is clearly identified with the voice of Jackie Kay as a young woman. In 'So You Think I'm a Mule', the voice is also Kay's, though the poem represents too the voice of a classmate: the person to whom the poem, including the dramatic closing line, is addressed. This voice may be based on a real person, but it's more likely a conglomeration of various people Kay knew. The poem is, at one level, addressed to a classmate who confronts the young Kay about her mixed race heritage, but it is also addressed to all white people, in a personal declaration of Kay's pride in being identified – despite her 'half white blood' – as 'pure black'.

'Mother Poem 2' is the most difficult to analyse in terms of identifying voices. Kay's voice is clearly present, and if we were in any doubt, she tells us on the cassette that this is one of a collection of poems called *The Adoption Papers* in which she attempts to give voice to her two mothers – her birth mother and her adoptive mother – and herself. But in analysing this poem, as in analysing the positionality of authors such as Ostriker and Rumens, Carter and even Showalter, it is necessary to go a bit deeper and look for other voices as well. Kay's 'self-representation' is contained in 'Mother Poem 2', but it is not one unified voice. Rather, Kay appears as the baby who was not available for adoption until the adoptive mother made it clear that she would 'not mind' having a black baby; she is present as the author of the poem (in the narrative voice which runs throughout), and she is also present as the 'subject' of the poem: the material of the poem's story is Kay's life, and she has both borrowed from her own life, and created fictional representations of it. The poem is a piece of fiction, based on facts woven together by Kay. Just as Jackie Kay is now a mother herself – with the consequence that her relationship to the concept of motherhood is now enriched by experience of mothering as well as of being mothered – so this poem is enriched by a multiplicity of voices, many of which are Kay's and some of which are fictional creations made by Kay.

As in the *Guardian* extract on Grace Nichols associated with Activity 23, this activity is concerned with making connections between the voices of women poets and of the women represented in their poems. Again, we cannot assume that the poet and the woman represented in any given poem are the same. One of the advantages of fiction writing (poetry, prose and drama) is the freedom to create new characters. Yet these poems by Jackie Kay are unusual in that they depict a real situation – Kay's adoption by white parents, and experiences growing up in the predominantly white community of Glasgow. Kay has created several characters, all based on her own experiences. Yet it would not be accurate to say that the women in the poems are 'real'. They have been created by Jackie Kay: they are voices emerging from a poem she has created. What she chose to include, and to exclude, to focus on and to ignore, has shaped the stories these voices tell. Kay's relationships with the four voices also influence the way they appear in their fictional form within the poems.

SUMMARY OF KEY POINTS ABOUT POETRY

If you compare the poems you have read and heard by Nichols and Kay to the pieces you have read by Ostriker and Rumens about the process of writing poetry, you will find that they share certain themes, including self-identity, women's sense of their own physical size and appearance, and birth as a creative and defining process in terms of women's sense of self. These four authors come from very different backgrounds in terms of class, as the educated middle-class 'voices' which emerge from the Ostriker and Rumens articles suggest. Perhaps more importantly, however, Ostriker and Rumens are white and Nichols and Kay are black. Therefore, when we think about poetry in relation to the authors' positions, we must consider the influences not only of gender, but also of race, class, privilege and differences in the experiences of the authors.

SET BOOK: *ON EARTH TO MAKE THE NUMBERS UP*

The articles you have read so far have either been fictional (the poems and short stories we have discussed) or have been about fiction (the Showalter, Goodman and Bonner essays, and the articles by Ostriker and Rumens about writing poetry). Now we are going to shift to a different but closely related form of literary representation: autobiography. Before we move on, it will be helpful if you go back to the beginning of this part of the Study Guide and review the list of key ideas and aims for this chapter (p. 24). You will need to be able to make the connection between these points as they have been illustrated in, and as they relate to, fiction, and the following material.

▶ ACTIVITY 25 ◀

You should by now have read Evelyn Haythorne's *On Earth to Make the Numbers Up*. Review any notes you may have made on that reading.

COMMENT

In reading Evelyn Haythorne's work, it may have occurred to you that autobiography, like poetry and women's writing about the process of writing poetry, is not purely non-fiction. It is a written representation of women's lives, influenced by the author's self-perception and position, background and status, as well as by gender, race, class and the politics of production and publishing in her cultural context.

You have encountered a form of autobiography earlier in the course: in the Course Introduction, when you heard a cassette on which three different women talked about their lives. But that kind of oral autobiography is very different from the written autobiography Haythorne offers in her book. Haythorne, like those three women, is a living woman whose real-life experiences are the material of our study. What all of these women choose to tell us, and how they tell it, will inevitably affect our way of seeing them and their lives. But it is important to make a distinction between women talking about their lives, and women writing autobiographies for publication. The style of published autobiography is bound to be more formal, more literary. Yet this kind of literature seems somehow more personal, less fictional, than do other forms of literature such as short stories and poetry.

ARTICLE 2.6 'CRITICISM AS AUTOBIOGRAPHY' BY NICOLE WARD JOUVE

You should now read Article 2.6 (pp. 113–115).

This short extract by Nicole Ward Jouve has been included here as a kind of bridge, to help you to make a mental connection between the critical ideas outlined by Showalter, the readings about fiction and poetry you have just dealt with, and the reading about autobiography which Wendy Webster provides. Rather than discuss the Jouve as an independent text, it is therefore most useful to examine it in relation to the essay by Wendy Webster.

ARTICLE 2.7 'OUR LIVES: WORKING-CLASS WOMEN'S AUTOBIOGRAPHY IN BRITAIN' BY WENDY WEBSTER

Please now read Article 2.7 (pp. 116–127).

We might stop and compare Ostriker's and Rumens' writing about their poetry to Nicole Ward Jouve's idea that criticism is a form of autobiography: that writing criticism requires making choices about inclusion and exclusion of 'facts', which is similar to the process of writing fiction, and which is also influenced by the author's perspectives and background (as influenced by gender, age, race, status etc.). The Ostriker and Rumens pieces deal not only with poetry as a form of literature, but also with the process of writing poetry based on personal experience. Similarly, Ward Jouve's short extract deals with the idea that writing criticism is like writing autobiographical literature, in the sense that the writer's background and ideas are so closely bound up in the kind of criticism she writes, and the way she writes it. By contrast, Wendy Webster's article on the subject of working-class women's autobiography takes a more academic (less personal) approach to the subject of women's lives, treating women's autobiography as literature, more similar in style to other forms of fiction and non-fiction, than to oral accounts of personal experience. We can think of working-class women's autobiography as a form of literary representation which is written by women as a means of expressing ideas and of painting pictures with words (remembering that all authors may omit words and images in order to give certain impressions, just as other words and images – real and imaginary – may be purposefully included).

CHAPTER 2 LITERARY REPRESENTATIONS: SELF AS SUBJECT

▶ **ACTIVITY 26** ◀

Listen to Audio-cassette 2, Side 2, 'Women's Autobiography', and do the activities included on that cassette.

COMMENT

The activities you have just done should serve to reinforce some of the ideas raised in the articles by Jouve and Webster. In hearing Evelyn Haythorne's voice as she read from her own work, we hope that you may have got the sense – as in hearing the voices of Jackie Kay and Grace Nichols reading their poetry on the other side of the cassette – that the author's voice and the narrative voice(s) within any given work can be very similar, but are not necessarily identical. Personal experience can infuse and inform literary works of various kinds, but it does so most directly in poetry and in autobiography. What is most interesting about autobiography is that, as a genre, it claims to represent the real lives of real people. In the case of working-class women's autobiography, it is working-class women's lives which we read and hear about. Yet it is only that which those women tell us: we do not know them in any full sense. In writing autobiographies, then, women write their own histories and 'write themselves out of exclusion' only to the extent that they want to. The subversive strategy of making art (literature) of their lives is not a mimetic one, but rather a creative process of selection and active self-representation.

▶ **ACTIVITY 27** ◀

Compare the two different approaches to autobiography which are outlined in the introduction to Chapter 2 in Book Four and exemplified in the readings by Nicole Ward Jouve and Wendy Webster (Jouve's on academic criticism as a kind of autobiography vs. Webster's on working-class women's autobiography as a type of social criticism). Summarize the main ideas of each approach. Then return to the introduction to Chapter 2 of *Imagining Women* and re-read the last two paragraphs on page 71, which discuss the relationship between the articles by Jouve and Webster. Is the relationship clear to you? Try to list the main points of similarity and difference between the two readings.

COMMENT

Obviously, the article by Wendy Webster is much longer than the one by Nicole Ward Jouve. As in discussion of the stories in *Wayward Girls and Wicked Women*, it is important to consider the intended context of these two articles. Ward Jouve's is an extract from a book on the subject of feminist literary criticism. It has been extracted and set in the context of your course materials, but was not originally intended to be used (read) in this context. By contrast, Webster's article was written for you. It was designed with the needs of your course in mind, and was used in preparation of Audio-cassette 2, Side 2. Both Webster's article and the cassette should prove very useful when you do your project.

The extract by Nicole Ward Jouve focuses on feminist criticism, and takes the view that in writing criticism, women express a good deal about themselves and their own positions, as well as about the material they set out to study and criticize. This short reading is extracted from a book called *White Woman Speaks with Forked Tongue: criticism as autobiography* (1991). Just as it was important in discussing Angela Carter's anthology to distinguish between the editor and the short story writers included, so it is important to make a similar point about the authorship of Jouve's book. Jouve is the author of the entire book: the introduction and all the essays which comprise its chapters. But that is not to say that her voice is homogeneous throughout. In fact, one of the central arguments of the book is that the personal voice of the author will vary with different subjects, and different styles of writing, though the position of the author will nearly always influence the writing to some extent. Jouve 'positions' herself on the first page of her book, in the preface, where she writes in her first sentence: 'No one who writes today can or should forget their race and their gender. The "I" who has written this book is white: privileged, yes, middle class, yes; and everything it has to say is limited and coloured by unconscious western European assumptions' (Jouve, 1991). By contrast, in Webster's article the emphasis is not on criticism as the chosen means of written expression of the educated middle class, but rather on the first-hand accounts of working-class women's lives.

Webster discusses autobiography as genre, and argues that it is the major genre in which women have written, and is also one of the lowest ranked in terms of a hierarchy of genre status (the novel and poetry, like traditional academic criticism, appearing near the top; 'women's writing' in all genres, and most popular writing including science fiction and romances, appearing near the bottom). But what is most interesting and compelling is Webster's observation (on p. 116) that one of the reasons why women write autobiography is related to its low status:

> It occupies a low place in the hierarchy of genres, so that it offered working-class women a form which did not involve claims to high artistic aspiration, and was often seen for that reason as appropriate for them to work in, in so far as writing was regarded as appropriate work at all.

The hierarchy of genres according to status is, of course, related to the valuing of women's work in many other fields. It is also related to class distinctions in other areas of society. Working-class women were, therefore, disadvantaged by their sex and their class in terms of access to education and language. As Webster notes, the 'belief that working-class women cannot and should not write has proved remarkably persistent', even today (p. 116). Evelyn Haythorne is one of a very few working-class women whose writing is known and studied. When we study the role and status of working-class women's writing, we therefore learn a great deal about the role and status of working-class women. Their autobiographies can be read, not only as literature, but also as a form of social criticism.

SUMMARY

You have now considered the relationship between author's voices and their forms of writing in a wide variety of forms of literary representation, including criticism, fiction (short stories and poems), and writing about writing (academic essays or articles such as Ostriker's about the process of writing poetry). The question about 'feminist writing versus women's writing' is relevant to all of these forms of writing.

You have now covered a great deal of material, and it may take some time before you feel you want to go on to read more poetry or fiction. But we hope that these activities will have engaged your interest in literary representations and that, in future, you may wish to read more fiction and autobiography. In particular, when you have finished this course and find a bit of spare time, you may want to go back and read Carter's *Wayward Girls and Wicked Women* and Haythorne's *On Earth to Make the Numbers Up* at a more leisurely pace. We chose these as set texts not only because they are worthy of study in relation to this course, but also because they are interesting books in their own right: worth keeping, reading and re-reading. Similarly, the Poetry Supplement which goes with this Study Guide contains many poems you may want to read again in future.

For now, however, it is most important that you have picked up on all the key points of this part. You might go back and review the list of key ideas and aims once more. But if you have got this far, the odds are that you have been following along and can make connections between the general theme of cultural representations and gender, and its expression – or various forms of expression – in literary representations of different kinds. In the next section, some of the same key issues will be discussed in relation to different forms of cultural representations: the plastic, representational, visual and craft-based arts. It will be helpful if you do not see the next section as a distinct and unrelated subject. In fact, the key ideas raised in the next section are very similar to those covered in this section. You would do well to take what you have learned here and apply it to your study of women's art making.

4
CHAPTER 3 VISUAL IMAGES: TAKING THE MASTERY OUT OF ART (WEEK 28)
(prepared by Catherine King)

The Hayward Gallery has never given a retrospective exhibition to any woman. The BBC has appointed six women to the 165 top jobs in its structure. In all the Art Colleges in the UK, only one Painting Department is headed by a woman. Out of the 71 Royal Academicians, six are women.

(Statistics gathered on the occasion of the campaign by the Labour Party, The Missing Culture 1987/1988: Women in the Visual Arts and Media)

During this week – Week 28 – you will be considering how the issues you have been thinking about in Weeks 26 and 27, with reference to spoken and written words, can be transferred to the visual and tactile arts. Here too you will find that women have been segregated to what are called lower genres, in, say, creating textiles, showing their accomplishments in watercolours, and not making things which are large, long-lasting and on permanent public display. As with literary representation, you will be considering the ever-changing feminist critical revolution, which has, so far, licensed us to revalue the products of all women and to trace the images of the first self-consciously feminist artists, from the 1850s onwards. Like science-fiction writers, women artists too have been able to envisage better worlds. Like women poets, artists also can explore ways of representing the taboo experiences of producing blood, milk and children. Do women do a disservice to themselves in failing to 'unfix' the stereotypes of the feminine, if they do show their physical and mental experiences as women? Or should women claim their full physically creative potential, along with their abilities as writers and artists, to be co-existent powers? What do women making art share with one another? How do categories such as race, religion, class and sexuality delineate the feminine? It seems that images and objects made by women of differing cultural locations require concomitantly different viewings, and certainly not a few minor adjustments to the lenses created for some supposedly 'core' white, heterosexual, western standpoint. There are many feminist garments to be designed and worn, but we must think of them as tailored to the wearers, and not made to fit by quick alterations to some 'unifem' off-the-peg clothing.

There are a number of key concepts you will want to bear in mind as you work on Chapter 3. These are:

the female gaze

the male gaze

a democracy of the gaze

mastery of the gaze

masculine visual ideology

objectification

the split subject

CHAPTER 3 VISUAL IMAGES: TAKING THE MASTERY OUT OF ART

By the end of this week of study you should be able to:

1. Consider and gain some appreciation of feminist views of women's visual and tactile arts.
2. Understand the way in which dominant ideologies achieve mastery of the gaze, in a masculine control of the institutions of production and consumption, with the result that womens' looking and self-representation is constrained (Articles 3.1 and 3.3 in particular).
3. Understand the ways in which women of varying cultural backgrounds create self-consciously self-defining images, which cannot be recuperated by dominant ideologies (Articles 3.2 and 3.4 in particular).

CHAPTER 3 INTRODUCTION

Please begin by reading the introduction to Chapter 3 (pp. 128–129).

In this introduction, King summarizes the way in which women's works have been demoted in historical accounts and critical writings, and the way in which women historians, critics and artists can oppose such definitions as 'the subordinate other'.

► **ACTIVITY 28** ◄

In Figure 7, I have mixed terms used by masculine historians and critics to 'describe' the work of women as 'opposed' to the work of men. To check that you have grasped how the system of control works, with respect to art, sort out the terms into their 'normal' pairs and groups under the headings 'Women's work' and 'Men's work', overleaf.

(Figure 7 contains the following terms arranged in a circle: by famous genius; home; collective production; traditional/conventional; to be paid for; professionally made; minor mistress; studio; Fine Arts; historically insignificant; an individual creation; stylistically and technically inventive; freely given; Great Master; crafts; of mainstream significance; by unknown artist; an amateur product)

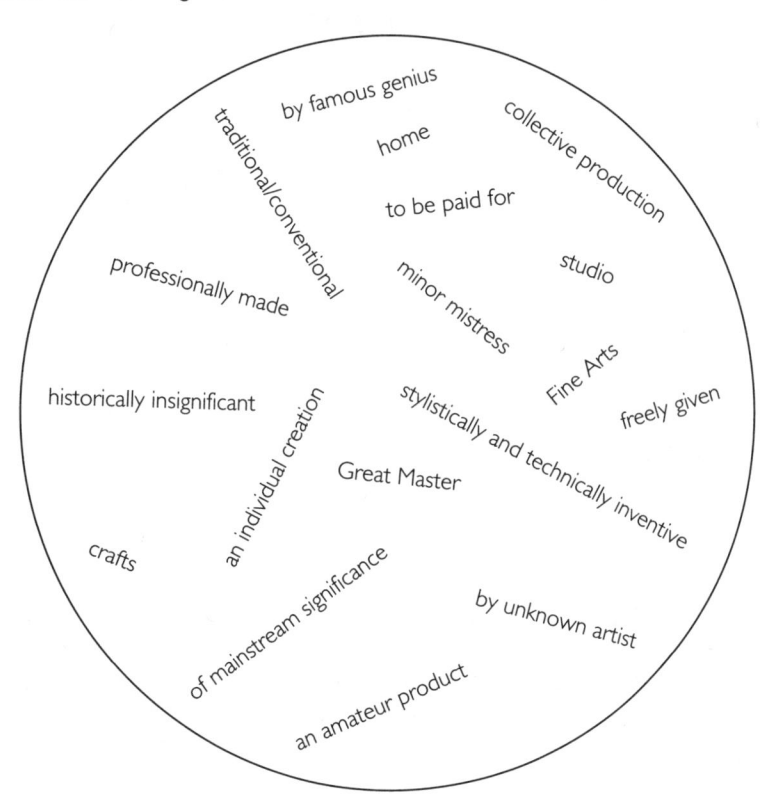

Figure 7

Women's work   **Men's work**

COMMENT
These are the listings I came up with:

Women's work	Men's work
crafts	Fine Arts
collective production	an individual creation
by unknown artist	by famous genius
historically insignificant	of mainstream significance
freely given	to be paid for
traditional/conventional	stylistically and technically inventive
an amateur product	professionally made
home	studio
minor mistress	Great Master

When I muddled the answers, I thought how artificial the pairs of supposed opposites were. Crafts could be described as individual creations. Works of great genius were supposed to be made for love, not for money or fame. So-called Fine Arts were often made collectively (like buildings, or large mural schemes) and so on. This is an extremely powerful set of binaries which condemn women's works as of only local, family, marginal interest. In this way, men's works are thrown into relief, as being significant, supposedly for all time and all the world – for Mankind. Men's works make up the 'canon' of classics to be imitated and matched.

How can feminists oppose these values? One approach has been to seek institutional changes so that women can enter into the ownership of a Fine Art training; become professional, well-paid, famous, mainstream image-makers; own galleries; run museums; teach art and art history; write art criticism and control investments in the art world. But as we start trying to write sentences saying 'women can become Geniuses, Great Masters ...', we begin to realize that this means so changing the words of art – its discourses – that the entire system of art making would have to change, along with its values. Only up to a certain point can women join the masculine institutions of Fine Art, and share in them, without disruption of so radical a nature that these institutions would cease to be 'Fine Art'.

Another group of approaches sets out, then, to alter the very discourses of art, rather than to imagine that women can wriggle across the masculine system of Fine Arts into the men's column. Theoretical analysis discloses the way the brilliance of masculine Fine Art, to make it visible at all, relies upon putting female crafts into the shade, into obscurity, and that, once women refuse to play their darkness to his masculine light, the latter disappears completely. Institutional change has to be accompanied by artists making things which review women's experiences and women's aims, as well as by historians and critics able to analyse past and present art production to disclose the joins in the seamless appearance of 'malestream' interpretation and judgement. New, more open and more flexible models must be proposed, to replace the lop-sided schemata of the past. It has been the power of women's images and women's theorizing that has shown up men's art, not as the objective truths of a mature humanity, but as just this: 'men's art'.

ARTICLE 3.1 'THE POLITICS OF REPRESENTATION: A DEMOCRACY OF THE GAZE' BY CATHERINE KING

Article 3.1 considers the second of the objectives for Chapter 3 and asks how dominant ideologies achieve mastery of the gaze and male control of the institutions of making and interpreting art, with the result that women's ability to represent themselves and others is constrained, as are their full rights to looking.

King begins by surveying different kinds of representations and proposing that we get used to the idea of using the term 'signifiers' and the phrase 'suggests the illusion of' to describe the more or less convincing ways in which artists allude to objects or ideas, so as to leave phrases like 'more or less realistic' to describe whether the objects alluded to ever existed, do exist, are legendary, or, indeed, are part of the imagination of the artist.

> To understand this point, please now read the first three paragraphs of Article 3.1 (pp. 131–133, as far as the paragraph beginning 'Similarly, the prestigious traditions ...'). Then read the next seven paragraphs (pp. 133–137, as far as the paragraph beginning 'Although all representation ...').

In these next seven paragraphs, King considers the way in which men pack the institutions controlling the creation and the interpretation of representations, to the virtual exclusion of women, so that there is a *tyranny* of the gaze, not a democracy. The silkscreen print by Tom Phillips, to which King refers and which appeared in *The Independent* on 18 April 1991, is shown here in Figure 8. Below is the 'advertisement' for it which appeared in the article on the sixth International Contemporary Art Fair, 'Art London 91', which accompanied the print:

> The biggest bargain of the Sixth International Contemporary Art Fair, "Art London 91" which was opened by the Duchess of York at Olympia last night, is on stand 639, **writes Geraldine Norman**.

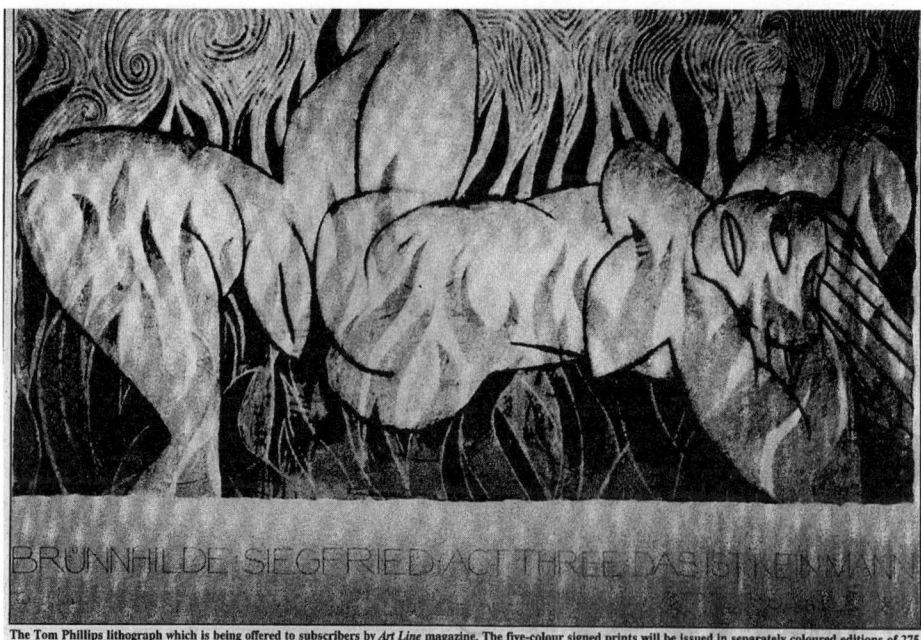

CHAPTER 3 VISUAL IMAGES: TAKING THE MASTERY OUT OF ART

Figure 8
'Artist gives magazine a line on raising cash' by Geraldine Norman,
The Independent, 18 April 1991

Art Line magazine is offering a free silkscreen print by Tom Phillips, worth about £500, to anyone who takes out a year's subscription – which will cost them £28, including postage.

(The Independent, *18 April 1991, p. 6*)

► **ACTIVITY 29** ◄

Now try out your grasp of the effects of the mastery of the male gaze by writing down briefly your response to the well-known painting *A Bar at the Folies Bergère* by the Great Master, Manet, shown in Figure 9. Can you summarize the two reactions a woman can opt for on seeing this painting?

Female gaze (1)   **Female gaze (2)**

CHAPTER 3 VISUAL IMAGES: TAKING THE MASTERY OUT OF ART

Figure 9
Edouard Manet, *A Bar at the Folies Bergère*, 1881–2, 95 x 130 cm.
Courtauld Institute Galleries, London, Courtauld gift 1934

COMMENT

I can try to respond to this image of a desirable woman, standing in the centre front of the painting, as if I were the imagined male client. I can try to imagine I can swagger in such a public masculine space, as master of what is laid out for my desire. I can try to imagine I am in the place from which the Great Master designed the image. But being a woman, imagination conflicts rapidly with the knowledge that I do not possess public space, will never be a Great Master, let alone a Great Connoisseur (masculine gender, French). I identify strongly with the painted woman who serves the master of the gaze. The response is, then, very fragmented.

Secondly, I can disregard trying to imagine I am a man when looking at this painting. I can look at it genuinely as a woman, fully acknowledging all the conflicts entailed in my first response and considering the painting critically as a representation working to promote certain responses in a male buyer, and certain notions about women. From this oblique angle, it looks more artful than Work of Art. From this position, I am in a stubborn, cynical mood. And I cannot, somehow, enjoy all that fine paint work, or figurative references to glass vessels and flowers because I have started to think of them as rows of women-sign-as-containers ... What did you put, I wonder? It is a little like trying to cut things with right-handed scissors if you are left-handed.

Please now read to the end of the article on page 139.

► **ACTIVITY 30** ◄

As you read, bear the following questions in mind and jot down brief answers (words, a phrase or two) in response:

(a) Can you define 'the democracy of the gaze'?

(b) What does 'objectification' mean? And how can it conflict with a democracy of the gaze?

Figure 10
'Give her your pay packet'. Photograph by Jill Posener, London 1982

COMMENT

(a) The phrase 'democracy of the gaze' aims at an ideal situation in which looking, interpreting and making images might go on in a more egalitarian way. In Article 3.4, King surveys the many different ways in which women have tried to demonstrate a fairer gaze (see especially Colour Plates 15 and 18 and Black and White Plates 15 and 18 in *Imagining Women*).

(b) 'Objectification' means representing a person as if they were an insentient thing, without human rights, so the word has an inegalitarian tendency. Looking around, we can see many degrees of objectification, from representations of goddesses, or a puppet woman mouthing her praise of a certain brand of soap flakes, to, say, Snow White.

The raising of consciousness concerning the effects of objectification, as well as the search for rights of representation have informed feminist art since the 1970s. An extract from a hand-out, produced by one of the artists you saw in Television Programme 01, *Feminist Strategies in Art*, illustrates the experiments going on in just one women-only life-drawing class in London:

Liberating Life Drawing is about how women as image makers and viewers relate to women as an object of the gaze/the sight. By challenging one's own way of drawing, the group believes that it can also challenge one's own way of seeing ... Even today, many life-drawing classes function, still, within a modernist framework which regards the female body as the 'ideal art form'. The problem with such a concept is that it gives women the role of 'model' and men the role of 'artist'. It also prevents the model from talking back, seeing and being. At a Liberating Life Drawing session one becomes rapidly aware that we are all women with voice and sight. Being of the same gender, we believe that the traditional power relationship: object of the gaze/maker can be broken. As women we all have experienced, culturally if not personally, being objectified by the male gaze.

(Françoise Dupré: Introduction to her group's exhibition 'Liberating Life Drawing: 1991'. Information on her group's class and exhibition kindly provided by the artist to the author at the time of the making of Television Programme 01, Autumn 1991)

ARTICLE 3.2 'OBJECT INTO SUBJECT: SOME THOUGHTS ON THE WORK OF BLACK WOMEN ARTISTS' BY MICHELLE CLIFF

Begin by reading the first eleven paragraphs of Article 3.2 (p. 140 as far as the break on p. 143), thinking about the way objectifications work to create and maintain racist stereotypes.

How, according to Cliff, are white women split from black women by male white dominant culture?

Whereas Article 3.1 looked at the objectifications and dichotomizing which segregate women from men, Michelle Cliff here analyses the way in which the same cultural system divides white from black women. White women can be persuaded to collude with white men in projecting onto black women the feared qualities with which they have themselves been stereotypically loaded: so that the black woman can be 'subordinate other' to the 'sacred *white* madonna'. In this way, black women have had the burden of being inferior others, culturally, both to men *and* to white women.

Now read the article to the end (on p. 153), thinking through these questions as you do so:

How do Edmonia Lewis's sculptures display the great problems for an artist from a sub-culture designing in the art forms of her Master Culture?

How did the task faced by Harriet Powers compare with that of Edmonia Lewis? Was it, in some ways, easier for Harriet Powers to make oppositional statements?

Michelle Cliff stresses that Edmonia Lewis negotiated the neo-classical sculptural style with great difficulty, because the favoured material, following Greek precedent, was white marble, and the favoured models of human beauty were also Greek. *Forever Free* is therefore a black woman's statement fettered by the peculiar artistic language in which she had to speak in order to obtain any audience at all. With *Hagar*, however, she had the brilliant idea of using an Old Testament analogy to offer a parable for the treatment of black women, and so to carry a powerful statement on the irreproachable and prestigious vehicle of biblical history.

Harriet Powers was excessively poor in comparison with Edmonia Lewis, and had a smaller audience. Arguably, though, she had an easier task, at least in expressing her views through the artistic skills of her own sub-culture – the appliqué quilts of the Fon people. Since Harriet Powers was using coloured pieces of cloth, she could show the Creation story in a colour coding which does *not* give us a white bible. Although Satan is black, we find that the other biblical actors are shaped in a variety of colours: white, grey, buff and speckled. In her Second Bible Quilt, she placed a metaphor for black women's freedom, in the centre base in her design, in her illustration of the escape of a sow called Betts: an 'independent hog, which ran 500 miles' from Georgia to Virginia (p. 150). This sow, like Adam, is made from grey-black cloth. Using an art form which belonged to women, as a derided craft, Harriet Powers was able to review the Bible in black terms, and to turn the image of black woman as beast-of-burden into a narrative of independent strength and comedy. Since she did this design for a group of white women (spouses to Boston University professors), she was speaking, self-consciously, to the 'mistress-culture'. Indeed, she placed an image of Job praying for his enemies as her first scene in this stitched story, as her statement of the black woman's magnanimous attitude to her enemies.

> **Further details about the quilts by Harriet Powers**
>
> *The First Bible Quilt* (Colour Plate 4 in *Imagining Women*), after 1886, reading from left to right, from the top: 1 Adam and Eve in the Garden of Eden; 2 Eve and Adam with their first born son, Cain; 3 Satan amidst the Seven Stars; 4 Cain has killed his brother Abel; 5 Cain travels to the land of Nod to find a wife; 6 Jacob dreams of the angels climbing the ladder to heaven; 7 the Baptism of Christ; 8 the Crucifixion; 9 Judas with the thirty pieces of silver; 10 the Last Supper; 11 the Nativity.
>
> This is how Harriet Powers described the Nativity scene: 'The next history is the Holy Family: Joseph, the Virgin and the infant Jesus with the Star of Bethlehem over his head. These are the crosses he had to bear through his undergoing. Anything for wisement. We can't go back any further than the Bible' (in Adams, n.d., pp. 27–8).
>
> *The Second Bible Quilt* (Colour Plate 5 in *Imagining Women*), reading from left to right, from the top: 1 Job praying for his enemies; 2 the Dark Day of 19 May 1780; 3 the serpent lifted up by Moses; 4 Adam and Eve in the garden; 5 John baptising Christ; 6 Jonah cast overboard; 7 the Creation of the animals, two by two; 8 *The Falling of the Stars*, 13 November 1833; 9 two of every kind of animal; 10 the Angels of Wrath and the seven Vials; 11 *Cold Thursday*, 10 February 1895: a man frozen at his jug of liquor; 12 *The Red Light Night*, 1846; 13 rich people who were taught nothing of God; 14 the Creation of animals; 15 the Crucifixion.

You should note that there are important links between this article and the views and images put forward by Rita Keegan and Zarina Bhimji in Television Programme 07 *Outside In*. Glance back at the Media Notes for this programme to see how Rita Keegan describes the cultural position of women of diverse cultural locations, working in Western Europe.

In the next article, we continue to consider the problematic strictures on women who claim rights to representing themselves.

ARTICLE 3.3 'BEYOND THE MIRROR: WOMEN'S SELF PORTRAITS' BY FELICITY EDHOLM

In Article 3.2, you were looking at representing the powers of black women against the stifling stereotypes of dominant white culture. In Article 3.3, Felicity Edholm focuses on women representing themselves in another personal sense, in making images of their own appearance, in self portraits. Given the commanding male gaze, a woman is made to see herself in a split fashion: a split between being a 'sight' (judged by men) and being one who sees and can make judgements herself. Where a woman portraying herself will be expected

CHAPTER 3 VISUAL IMAGES: TAKING THE MASTERY OUT OF ART

to consider whether she looks pleasing and desirable to men, a man portraying himself will consider himself as an entire judge of his own appearance, and can show himself as one who is to be pleased and who desires.

Please begin reading Article 3.3 now, up to the heading 'Women and Self Portraiture' (pp. 154–161).

▶ **ACTIVITY 31** ◀

As you read these paragraphs:

(a) List the traits of images of women, as opposed to those of men, which offer us exemplary models of femininity.

(b) What conventions of portrayal and self-portrayal have been available in the Western European and North American traditions of art for women to use as artists? Can you think of examples of portraits/self portraits of women which fall into the three categories listed by Felicity Edholm?

(a) Exemplary models	
Female images are shown as	Male images are shown as

(b) Conventions of female portraiture

This is what I came up with:

(a) Exemplary models	
Female images are shown as	Male images are shown as
1 white	1 white
2 anonymous face and body	2 individuated, or named persons
3 completed by men and children	3 apparently self-sufficient
4 passive	4 active, in authority
5 defined in relation to men (not other women)	5 defined in relation to their status with regard to other men

(b) Conventions of female portraiture		
1 Commemorative portrait as displaying social status and dignity	2 Portrait as 'revealing' of personality and character	3 Portrait which stands for an admirable trait in humanity
Examples:	Examples:	Examples:
Whistler's mother; Hogarth's daughters; Florence Nightingale on bank notes; Portraits of Elizabeth I/Queen Victoria	Portraits of Charlotte Brontë, Elizabeth Barrett Browning	Alice Walker as Muse Thalia: of Comedy (see Colour Plate 1 in Book Four); Gwen John's six portraits of the founder of the Dominican convent at Meudon, Mère Poussepin

As Felicity Edholm stresses, women are, in general, offered restricted examples to follow within this tradition, which normally present women as (a) relations of men, not to be commemorated in their own right; (b) lacking that 'full individuality' which would justify a strikingly characterful portrait (it is typical of this form of representation that I could only think of two women writers here); and (c) such secondary humans that they are unable to convey the greatness of 'mankind' adequately.

> Please now continue reading Felicity Edholm's article up to the heading 'Käthe Kollwitz, 1867–1945' on page 163.
> What sorts of psychological experiences special to women inform a woman looking in a mirror and painting or drawing a resulting self portrait?

Children come to consciousness of their selves through becoming aware of the value that is placed on them by others, reflected in the reactions and behaviour of other people towards them (the things others say, the things a child is given to eat, wear or play with, and is approved of doing). A girl can compare these reflections with the treatment given to boys. She can also compare the reflections she gets from her prime carer (usually her mother) with that of her other carers. In societies which make mirrors (and self-portrayal can include the face/use illusionistic means), the different experience of women in relation to mirrors can mesh with the practices of self-portrayal. In the mirror you are offered the chance to see yourself, in some sense, as others see you (admittedly reversed and from one viewpoint), whereas, otherwise, you know yourself 'from inside'. How you read your reflection in the mirror will be informed by all the other social and physical reflections you have got and are getting from things and persons. Girls are treated differently from boys in a lop-sided nurturance pattern, where father stands for full external authority and mother stands for private relative authority. Girls must identify with mother and accept relative authority to become women. Boys can identify with full external authority to become men. So women see with relative authority and as if mentally looking over their shoulders in order to consider how those with full public authority judge them. They look at themselves being looked at.

> Now read to the end of Felicity Edholm's article on page 172 and consider the ways in which Käthe Kollwitz, Frida Kahlo and Suzanne Valadon worked with, and challenged, conventions of portraying women, in the role of split-subject enforced by a patriarchal society.

ARTICLE 3.4 'FEMINIST ARTS' BY CATHERINE KING

We end your work on this chapter by considering the short history of feminist arts and by looking at what has been the most successful feminist art so far.

> Please read the first seven paragraphs of Article 3.4 as far as the paragraph beginning 'When, in 1969, women ...' (pp. 173–176), in which King proposes that from the 1850s onwards, feminists adopted the strategies of (1) diverting feminine craft 'accomplishments' to state women's rights, or (2) appropriated masculine methods and forms to subvert them into statements of women's political views.

► **ACTIVITY 32** ◄

Can you give one example of each strategy, and write short notes on how both collapse the masculine system of the arts?

COMMENT

For the use of crafts to carry feminist ideas, you might have cited the American Women's Rights Quilt; the suffragette scarf of Janie Terreno, 1912; or other suffragette embroidery on banners or clothing. The taking over of men's Fine Arts by women was exemplified in the satirical drawing by Barbara Leigh-Smith, and the oil painting of Florence Claxton. The entire suffragette campaign used methods employed by male trade unions and political parties. Sojourner Truth's use of portrait photographs would count here too. I think that it is not just *what* women stated which was disruptive, but, crucially, the way they defied the dichotomies of 'separate spheres' in art. Women claimed the fields of Fine Art and public presence on the streets and squares. And they also made feminine quilts and scarves into political statements.

CHAPTER 3 VISUAL IMAGES: TAKING THE MASTERY OUT OF ART

First wave feminist artists set important precedents for pulling the carpet from under the feet of the hierarchy of the arts. But it was only second wave feminist artists who explicitly insisted on equality in the valuing and making of craft objects and visual images, so that democratic practices might become the ideals in training for the arts: the rights of artists, models, purchasers and users of art. Indeed, if you look back to my answer to Activity 28, you will find that the feminist artists of the 1970s and 1980s have placed the most positive value upon the (derided) practices listed in the column under 'women's work'.

Now please read paragraphs 8–12 as far as the paragraph beginning 'With knowledge of the US precedents ...' (pp. 176–180).

► **ACTIVITY 33** ◄

The article could only touch on a few of the ebullient ideas of the leading North American artists who began the second wave of feminist art. Can you jot down a few phrases and adjectives which characterize their bold ideas?

COMMENT

1 Collective/collaborative making, involves users of art.
2 The arts of the home (cooking, textiles, cleaning, slimming) are put forward as full arts, while the Studio Arts can move into the household.
3 Women can be represented as powerful (in myth, or, say, in traditionally male jobs).
4 Women seek their own femaleness supposedly behind the distortions of the male gaze, as if there were some essential woman to discover.
5 Women try to represent men in equality, not as helpless objectifications.

Now read the rest of the article, excluding the last three paragraphs (as far as the paragraph beginning 'In the exhibition ...', pp. 180–186). (There are many names and titles here, but the main thing to come away with is a sense of the diversity of feminist arts during this very creative period: and, of course, it is all going on still.)

Finally, turn to and read the conclusion to this article (pp. 186–188). King presents here four works which meet her criteria of successful feminist arts. These criteria are:

1 That the work self-consciously sets out to make women prime viewers.
2 That the image cannot be recuperated by dominant masculine ideology.

> **Further explanation of 'recuperation'**
> **Recuperating by dominant visual ideologies**
>
> To understand the way ideology could operate in democracies in which a large majority of subjects must be made to accede to the mythologies expressing the interests of the shifting allegiances of a small number of governing groups, the term 'hegemony' has been coined. (This term was used originally to define a group of confederate Greek city states in which one city held dominance over the majority.) The concept of hegemony alludes to the way in which ideologies must continue to accommodate these shifting allegiances and interests of the governing groups, and any external factors such as war, as well as silencing any oppositional readings of the meanings of social life from the majority. A variety of tactics appear available to allow the controllers of cultural production to carry on engendering meanings. One response is the description of feminist visual statements as 'dangerous social deviance'. The public outrage in 1973 at Monica Sjoo's painting of *God Giving Birth* would be an example of this. Another strategy entails the commodification of an oppositional visual statement, such as making very short hair-cuts, and dungarees, into fashionable styles for women. What begins as a minority rejection of marketed sexuality is turned back into 'feminine attractiveness' for the mass market. Further, resort can be had to 're-framing' or 'recuperating' feminist readings of art, so that some of what is new appears to be admitted as interesting or useful, while actually the values still follow the masculine routes. An illustration of this would be a willingness to publish *slim* biographies (monographs) of women who were painters, with very *attractive colour* plates, leaving intact the ideologies that an artist without the prefix is a man ('artist' as opposed to 'woman artist'), and that the *real business* of art history is the study of individual geniuses of which ('unfortunately, sorry Ladies') history *provides* us with many more men than women. (Note the way in which women are put into ideological positions where *history is giving them answers* at a level so basic that they just cannot question it.)
>
> King argues that some feminist images can refuse all attempts at re-framing. They seem to attain recalcitrance because their meanings are marked on them with words. This is not to say that the viewer does not make them hers or his, in looking at them, but that negotiation of interpretation is limited. It may seem bizarre that feminist visual and tactile art needs to be, partly, verbal. Perhaps the reason *why* this is so, at least at present, is that the mass of (men's) images arrive with the unspoken, unwritten discourses of men's mythology, men's religion and men's histories, pervading them. (There are strong links between this article and Television Programme 01 *Feminist Strategies in Art*. You might like to look at the Media Notes for this programme at this stage, to see what the artists say for themselves.)
>
> This article ends with an illustration of one of the posters made by The Guerrilla Girls. This is a US collective which designs hard-hitting and amusing poster art, to castigate the controllers of private and public galleries in New York whom they identify as sexist and racist. Like guerrilla fighters, they are unidentifiable, and are able to use surprise tactics of a great variety, to confuse the opposition who cannot hit back at an anonymous target.

We end this section with a rigorous argument which presents tough criteria for the most oppositional feminist art. But it would be wrong to think of setting up yet another hierarchy – this time in women's art – like that of men, with recalcitrant feminist pieces at the top. After all, there would not be any point in such recalcitrant examples if they were not claiming our rights to make

Figure 11
Mrs Lough, well-known Durham quilter. Photograph: The North of England Open Air Museum, Beamish, County Durham

anything, anywhere we please, as women. Therefore, I am going to end this week's work with two glimpses of the kind of women's works which the feminist revolution in artistic values has given us to celebrate.

QUILTING: SOME WOMANLY NEEDS IN THE NORTH-EAST

Hundreds, perhaps thousands, of wholecloth quilts were made in the North-East of England between 1870 and 1930. Some were workaday pieces but many are impressive and some are exceptional, with designs at once dense and sumptuous as the fine stitching throws the spaces between the lines into relief and gives the cheap Roman cotton sateen, from which they were commonly made, a soft sheen. The resulting effect is one of great luxury. Yet they were not made for stately homes or by well-to-do women. Many were made in pit villages and graced the beds of small back-to-back terrace houses.

After the first shock of pleasure such quilts give, what makes them memorable for me and reawakes my feelings, is a sense of how they fitted into the lives of the women who made them and the needs they satisfied for them. Though various sources have provided this information oral testimony figures prominently and importantly. The accretion of meaning these quilts have thus acquired is now both a source of, and inseparable from, the aesthetic response they arouse in me.

Life in the pit village

Life in the North-East pit villages was tough, not only physically but psychologically,

> My father was injured in the mines and he was denied compensation because the then doctor said his injury was due to natural disease. But he never worked again after the accident. The roof of the pit fell in on him and he was brought home battered and bruised from head to foot. And one bruise on his hip it didn't get better. It got worse ... he had to have one operation after another and he was left with a short leg. So, after that my mother stuck to quilting, in about 1925, to help us out with the housekeeping. *(Miss Shepherd)*

Women's lives were harsh. Masculinity was frequently expressed aggressively through brawling and drunkenness. And men generally expected a lot of attention,

> There was one old neighbour who used to come in. She'd say 'I've tellt wor Geordie ah wanted to com along and help Lizzie wi'ya quilt,' And she never put a stitch in! But she had that excuse to get out for an hour or two y'see. Husbands were very demanding in those days. *(Miss Shepherd)*

Quilting could be hard work if you did it for money. And quilts take an enormous number of hours. Yet quilting was frequently associated with a respite from work, with the warmth of companionship and the gleeful delights of conversation – even if an occasional acidity and bickering crept in. For many of their makers quilts became inextricably bound up with pleasurable memories.

> We always used to meet about two o'clock and hope to work till four, then stop and have a cup of tea. And we used to make scones ... and a sandwich cake ... and we would share it out. Those who didn't have to rush home to get their husbands' or their workers' meal in the evening would stay on where there was room ... We used to enjoy it. All the tales that were told over the quilting frame. Well, you could imagine. Everything was discussed! It was really entertainment making quilts as well as doing something useful. *(Mrs Little)*

Quilt designs

Quilting designs were also redolent of intimate and familiar surroundings,

> My mother had a lot of quilting patterns just at her finger tips. She just drew them freehand. When she was tired of a pattern, she would look around. She would copy anything that she would see, a curtain pattern, or a chair seat pattern. And people always liked the designs ... *(Miss Shepherd)*

Or again:

> Now on the coastline they had designs pertaining to the sea, seaweed and shells ... quite different ... to the designs that we had near the hills. Ours were all flowers and foliage and feathers. *(Mrs Snaith)*

Williamson talks about the way the women of this area established standards for themselves through the execution of certain household chores. His grandmother and her neighbours kept shining windows and derived a sense of self-respect from this. Opulent quilts could also create a sense of achievement and dignity.

The scope quilts offered for the play of creativity and imagination also provided for additional levels of satisfaction. Quilting became a form of visual language in which women recorded their responses to the world they found themselves in.

The front, back and interfacing of a quilt have to be secured for practical purposes. But the density of the quilting in wholecloth quilts invariably goes far beyond practical requirements. It becomes an essential element of the best quilts' opulence, by creating that surface ripple which subtly softens all the hard lines of the pattern and produces the play of light which makes quilts so eminently caressable. Another feature of these designs is the juxtaposition of sinuous, flowing lines and tight, close, straightline quilting. Much of the quilts' effect derives from the way the borders curve and beckon to the middle but at the same time are held in check by the straightline quilting.

Wholecloth quilts constitute a space in which harmony reigns and the senses are flattered. Both oral and other evidence shows that much of the life in the back to back terrace houses of mining villages was not like that. But to create such a vision cannot be interpreted simply as escapism. Against the world of these women, the handling of these patterns become material evidence of a strength of spirit which has resisted subjugation. The ebullience of the finished quilts reflects a human wilyness which, even under the most unprepossessing circumstances, finds the means for sensual gratification and a way of introducing luxury into one's life. This finally seems to be what these quilts are about. If one wants an argument for the value of art, here is one. The part oral history can play in developing such an interpretation is also clear.

(Freeman, 1990, pp. 27–8)

IN THE SHADE OF THE AVOCADO TREE, THE GIRL NEXT DOOR AND ME

Childhood memories. Grandmother's yard in Nigeria. Sitting under the huge avocado tree. Watching the girl next door plaiting head after head and eavesdropping on the latest gossip. Maintaining as unobtrusive presence as possible or I'd be sent away at the juicy bits. Wonderfully entertaining afternoons. Everyone off home with a truly individual style for a tip of a few pennies.

Gradually I started paying attention to the actual plaiting itself. I remember vividly my first plait. There I was fiddling with my hair as I watched television. I suddenly discovered that I could plait too. My sleeping sister was dragged from bed so I could practise on her hair. What a mess! But from there on there was no stopping me.

Saturdays in our house became the day all the girls in the neighbourhood came round to get their hair done for school. All very much a social event. Not the mainly commercial one it is nowadays, especially in the West.

My chosen career is science. While studying industrial science at Paisley College of Technology I found myself working occasionally in Hairlynks, a black hairdressing salon in Glasgow ...

I prefer plaiting at home as there is less pressure to perform. I don't have the salon's reputation to protect. As a result I am more relaxed, work faster and enjoy the gossip like the old days. Plaiting in a salon puts a different emphasis on the activity altogether. From being a social event of little or no economic value it has become a commercial enterprise. It often provides a good percentage of the income of any salon offering the service.

Whether or not that is a good thing depends on your point of view. Plaiting is detached from its cultural aspects. The provision of a significant service to the community is done at a price as opposed to almost free.

Traditionally the art of hairdressing in Africa was a woman's skill. Practised almost exclusively by women and generally for women. Plaiting a head of hair can take any length of time. However, most take an average of five hours to produce about seventy plaits ...

(Morgan, in Sulter, 1990)

CHAPTER 3 VISUAL IMAGES: TAKING THE MASTERY OUT OF ART

Figure 12
Plaiting, photographic sequence from Yemi Morgan, 'In the Shade of the Avocado Tree, the Girl Next Door and Me', in *Passion: discourses on blackwomen's creativity*, edited by Maud Sulter, 1990.
Photograph: Ingrid Pollard

5
CHAPTER 4 NEGOTIATING MEANINGS FROM POPULAR TELEVISION AND FILM (WEEK 29)
(prepared by Frances Bonner)

This part of the Study Guide, like this part of the book, moves from a consideration of texts which are made *by* women, and even predominantly feminist in their construction, to look at texts which are made *for* women, but rarely by them. The emphasis shifts with this to the audience and the way in which we as audience members take and make meaning from texts. There are two main reasons for this shift when dealing with this particular material. First, mainstream films and television programmes are probably the major sources of cultural representations for contemporary audiences. Second, more critical work, and more feminist critical work, has been conducted on mass media audiences than on those for visual or print art works.

The articles you will be reading and working with this week refer to a number of different films and television programmes, some of which you will probably be familiar with, some you may have some memory of having seen and some of which you may never have encountered. Obviously, if you can hire a video of *Coma* or *She's Gotta Have It* from your local shop and watch it, you will gain a deeper insight into the authors' arguments, but I realize this might not be possible for some students. The important arguments of the articles and the activities you will be asked to do during this week do not depend on familiarity with specific texts. These texts are examples from which I want you to grasp some general points. You will also find that Television Programme 08, *Taking the Credit: women in TV*, is particularly relevant to this part of the course.

At various points during the week I will ask you to think about or watch some television. If you are without access to a television set, try to do the same activity for radio. When the activity is a major one, a formal alternative will be suggested.

By the end of the week, you should:

- Be able to use the concept of negotiation to talk about how meaning is constructed and pleasure taken from texts.
- Understand why and how differently situated people take different meanings from the same text.
- Recognize the gender implications of the castigation of soap opera and game shows.

The first article, by Christine Gledhill, provides the main arguments on which the week's work is based, so be prepared to spend most time on this. You should also allow some time for re-reading the main introduction to *Imagining Women*.

CHAPTER 4 INTRODUCTION

Please begin by reading the introduction to Chapter 4 (pp. 190–192). This traces some of the changes that have occurred in feminist study of film and television and points out how initial work looked at the paucity of roles for women in film and television.

ACTIVITY 34

Is this still the case? Think of the non-fictional television programmes (news, game shows, sport, nature documentaries, arts programmes, chat shows etc.) that you watch and quickly list the people who appear regularly in them. How many are male and how many female? Who is on screen most? Who appears in control of what happens? And, when a man and a woman are on screen together, does the man speak to the viewers and the woman speak to the man on screen with her?

COMMENT

The early work was concerned with questions like these and you will probably have found that this type of analysis still reveals a televisual world in which men are considerably more likely to appear and to be in control.

In films, the situation may have become worse. The article from *The Guardian* reproduced below provides data on women and film which includes an extra basis for comparison – even when they are stars, women are paid less than men.

> Meryl Streep is paid half as much as male stars, and only one in 45 films this summer had a female lead. **Christopher Reed** on misogyny in movieland
>
> **SECOND-CLASS SUPERSTARS**
>
> Hollywood's bias against women, both in front of and behind the camera, has been revealed in a survey of eight major studios. It found that not one had a woman with the power to give final production approval, and that in 45 films released this summer only one had a female lead.
>
> The survey by the Los Angeles times examined Columbia, MGM-UA, Paramount, 20th Century Fox, Universal, Warner, Orion and Tri-Star. Altogether they offered 62 presidential and vice-presidential posts of which women held 22. Although many of these included putting the essential components of a film together, none was able to "green light", or give final authorisation.
>
> Among the 45 films examined, only Columbia's hit, Post-cards From The Edge, had female leads: Shirley MacLaine and Meryl Streep. Even more unusually, it was a story about women. Of the rest, only 16 contained what the Times team of critics and film writers regarded as significant parts for women. Among them was the romantic fantasy Ghost with Demi Moore, the year's highest-grossing movie.
>
> Yet despite such good box-office, women command less money. Oscar-winner Meryl Streep complains that she receives half the fees in comparable roles going to Dustin Hoffman, Robert Redford, or Jack Nicholson. "I think it stinks," she says.

Work for actresses in Hollywood has actually been declining since Streep became a star. Figures from the Screen Actors' Guild show that women now command only 29 per cent of all feature film roles and that those over age 40 are cast in less than nine per cent. In 1984 women won 34 per cent of all movie roles.

In Hollywood's 78-year history, only three women have been in charge of production: Dawn Steel at Columbia, Sherry Lansing at Columbia and Fox, and Paula Weinstein, whose vice-presidency of production at Warner Bros 15 years ago was Hollywood's first such appointment. But none lasted more than three years at the top and only Steel was responsible for both the creative and business side of the studio.

A fourth, the late Lucille Ball, was chief of her own studio, Desilu. Although that dealt mainly with television productions, she did introduce technical innovations that advanced the art of film.

So the record of women in the industry is proven. Why do they still do so relatively poorly? Opinions range from flat accusations of sexism, to pleas of ignorance about how bad it has become, to commercial rationalisations from the industry itself.

Hollywood has always been a white male haven. Marc Kelly, director of Women in Film, a research group, says: "Men are commissioning scripts, finding scripts, writing, and directing them. Men are telling stories from their perspective, so women's voices are not being heard, period."

The Guild, which held a conference on the problem last August, is cautiously optimistic. Spokesman Harry Medved says that executives were simply not aware of how "depressing" the figures on women in film had become. Alerted by the conference, he added, many went away with verbal promises of casting more females, especially in minor characters such as a doctor or a taxi driver. Next year may demonstrate their sincerity.

As it is show "business", commercial criteria are paramount. The orthodox wisdom is that women are not as powerful a box-office magnet as men. Their appeal has also been declining since the starstruck days when their fame rested on surnames alone: Garbo, Crawford, Davis, Stanwyck.

By 1961 there were three women in the top 10 box-office draws: Elizabeth Taylor, first; Doris Day third; Sandra Dee sixth. In 1981 Dolly Parton was fourth; Jane Fonda fifth; Bo Derek eighth, and Goldie Hawn ninth. Last year only Kathleen Turner was listed – at No 10. But as Shirley MacLaine has remarked on the notion that women cannot "open" a film (pack in audiences over the vital first weekend): "That's because we don't have a chance at subjects that are profitable. It's a case of chicken and egg."

Two causes for women's decline in movies are contained in today's preponderance of action films. These attract the new mass audience – undiscriminating youngsters whose repeat visits create formula blockbusters. These are mainly "body count" action films with minimal dialogue. With their appeal to macho cultures they are especially rewarding in overseas sales, which now account for more than half of total receipts.

As women do not fit into these action sagas, they are less "marketable", the argument goes. Yet recent successes such as Steel Magnolias, with six female leads, Driving Miss Daisy, with an octogenarian female lead, and Sigourney Weaver's $4 million-plus percentage for Alien III, prove otherwise.

In the end money, not ethics or art, motivates Hollywood, and this season's body-count movies, Another 48 Hours, Die Hard 2, and RoboCop 2, did not do as well as expected. Perhaps Hollywood will now "discover" women – again.

(The Guardian, *22 November 1990, p. 28*)

CHAPTER 4 NEGOTIATING MEANINGS FROM POPULAR TELEVISION AND FILM

The article points out that twenty-two out of sixty-two presidential and vice-presidential posts in the major Hollywood studios are held by women:

> Why can it still claim that Hollywood is 'biased' against women?
>
> What arguments does it suggest for the decline in the number of female box-office draws?

You may like to think of more recent 'box-office hits' and whether the situation has changed, as the end of the article suggests.

The quotation on page 191 of Book Four, from Teresa de Lauretis, mentions a more recent concern for feminist scholarship in this area – that of constructing 'another (object of) vision and the conditions of visibility for a different social subject'. This will be more our concern for the rest of the week.

ARTICLE 4.1 'PLEASURABLE NEGOTIATIONS' BY CHRISTINE GLEDHILL

> Please read Article 4.1 through for a first time (pp. 193–209). The most important concept that the article advances is that of 'negotiation'. As you read, concentrate on this. Why does Gledhill think it is useful? What does she mean by it?

Gledhill argues (and I do find her very persuasive) that negotiation avoids a view of cultural production that gives total power over the production of meaning to the text. Instead, she sees meaning being produced by the processes of production and reception in what she terms both 'negotiation' and 'struggle'. You may care to ponder for a moment on why she chooses to use 'negotiation' as her principal term. I suspect it is because 'struggle' is related to physical aggression. Perhaps you recall previous instances in the course where the use of terms referring to physical conflict have been rejected.

The last paragraph of the early section 'Culture as Negotiation' (pp. 195–196) is important, but rather compressed. You will need to read it more than once. It opposes the ideas of 'dominant ideology' and 'hegemony' on the basis that the first involves the imposition of power, consciously or unconsciously, while the second argues that power involves persuasion as well as force – that there is an element of give-and-take in the maintenance of power. It is the second of these that underlies Gledhill's conception of 'negotiation'.

She sees negotiations as operating institutionally, textually and at the point of reception – that is, in the audience itself where it 'allows space to ... [our] subjectivities, identities and pleasures' (p. 199). Her analysis of the television series *Cagney and Lacey* provides a practical example of how these negotiations may occur institutionally and textually. If you are familiar with the programme, you may like to think about what aspects of it you find pleasurable and why (and if not, why not).

As I understand what Gledhill means by 'negotiation', it refers to the process whereby 'meaning' is made of a text from a combination of the cues it provides and the ways we understand them. It is something that is both conscious and unconscious, that involves decisions by those making the programmes and by those viewing them at home, to call on or refer to a number of various reading positions, genres, cultural signs and definitions. It serves the industry by maximizing audiences but also serves audiences by making it possible for representations and desires that they hold important to be called on and acknowledged.

> Now read the article for a second time.

Figure 13
Sharon Gless and Tyne Daly in *Cagney and Lacey*.
Photograph: John Kobal Collection

► **ACTIVITY 35** ◄

Gledhill suggests on page 194 that there is a problem in the relationship of the feminine spectator and the female audience. On page 205 she restates it as being between 'symbolic and referential roles'. Outline briefly what you think is meant by these terms.

COMMENT

The feminine spectator/symbolic role is constructed by the text and is more difficult to be certain of than the female audience which is constructed instead by factors such as gender, race and age, to which we may feel more secure about referring, however unrepresentative we may feel ourselves to be.

► **ACTIVITY 36** ◄

On page 206, Gledhill discusses the particular pleasures available in *Coma* from looking at Susan Wheeler/Geneviève Bujold's body. This relates to a lot of material you have already considered about the female and male gaze, and this may be a good point at which to re-read the section on the look and the gaze in the introduction to *Imagining Women*. Gledhill suggests that there is no role for the feminine spectator in the scenes where Susan is in the shower and at the aerobics class, but that members of the female audience may be able to negotiate a position in which they/we are able to take pleasure from what is on the screen. Outline the basis on which Gledhill makes this distinction.

COMMENT

When the camera 'looks' at Susan taking a shower, there is no place within the film for the feminine spectator, since such a person/position is not perceived as having any basis on which to gain pleasure from a desire for the woman's body. Gledhill, however, suggests that there are other bases on which members of the female audience can gain pleasure from this. They/we can identify with and enjoy the plot situation in which Susan has demanded and gained access to the shower ahead of her lover and left him frustrated by this. In a similar way, the aerobics class provides the possibility for us to recognize an acknowledgement of the pleasure women get in being together in specifically female social spaces. Gledhill is careful to point out that the film does not make either scene as specifically patriarchal or feminist, but that they are moments where negotiation occurs.

ARTICLE 4.2 'SHE'S GOTTA HAVE IT: THE REPRESENTATION OF BLACK FEMALE SEXUALITY ON FILM' BY FELLY NKWETO SIMMONDS

► **ACTIVITY 37** ◄

Before you read Article 4.2, look at the still from *She's Gotta Have It*, included in Book Four (Plate 20). Jot down briefly what you think the shot is trying to convey about the relationship between the two characters. How is it doing this? I will ask you to refer back to these notes after reading the article.

The director of *She's Gotta Have It*, Spike Lee, is widely credited with having demonstrated to mainstream Hollywood producers, with this film and his next, *Do the Right Thing*, that films made by and about young urban black men were profitable. The result was that a large number of such films began to be made and released at the beginning of the 1990s. At the time of my writing (November 1991), only one film by a young black American woman, Julie Dash's *Daughters of the Dust*, had been released – but only in 'art' cinemas – apparently in the light of these successes. (Actually, Dash had been researching the film for five years and its concern is emphatically non-urban.)

> Now read Article 4.2 (pp. 210–220), keeping in mind what Gledhill wrote about 'negotiation'. What negotiations are referred to in production terms?

Simmonds talks about how the film was created out of various impulses, attitudes and beliefs: Spike Lee's reactions to Alice Walker's views on black men and the popularity of these views with white audiences; from the slave owners' perception of the black woman as a breeder of a labour force; and from the attitudes of the men dominant in the black liberation movement of the 1960s, that the only role for a black woman was to be a possession of a black man. She also indicates Lee's desire to make a cheap and profitable film and his belief that a film ostensibly about black female sexuality was the way to do this. (He was, incidentally, right. The film was very cheap to make and very profitable.)

Simmonds points to the rape scene as central to the film's construction and representation of black female sexuality. You may have been surprised that a film could include a scene in which the lead character is raped and still be described as an 'erotic comedy' or, as in the part of the caption that was removed for its reprint here, a 'crackling modern romantic comedy'. Perhaps you have seen the film and recall being surprised at the inclusion of the scene. This is not a scene which I believe can be negotiated by a female audience to provide a non-patriarchal meaning. It demonstrates that the concept of negotiation does not imply that there is a free-for-all in the production of meanings by audiences. There are constraints and there are instances where the space for negotiation is quite slight.

► **ACTIVITY 38** ◄

Look again at the still from *She's Gotta Have It* (Plate 20) and at the notes you made in response to Activity 37 before reading the article. Perhaps you had seen the film and thus knew something about the plot, or perhaps even so, you had forgotten about the rape scene. I know that when I think of the film, I recall other, less unpleasant, moments first. Do you want to change your assessment of the relationship now that you are aware that the man gazing in such a concerned way (or that is how I read the picture) will, later in the film, rape the woman he is looking at? Note any changes in your interpretation.

COMMENT

The changes that may have occurred in your reading of the still will result not only from your knowledge of what is to happen between the two people later in the film, but also from the other plot details that Simmonds' article has provided. You may have placed greater emphasis on the way Nola has wrapped the bedclothes so tightly about her thighs and is resolutely not looking at Jamie. You may have paid more attention to the candles and the 'altar' bed. In both the early and the later readings of the still you will probably have referred to the way in which the 'look' inside the film – from Jamie at Nola – directs our gaze through male eyes. As you will have gathered from reading Simmonds, this is characteristic of the film. The camera's gaze is indeed a male gaze, but as well as being gendered, it is also racially located. It is a black male gaze.

> How does Simmonds suggest that this black male gaze is distinctive?
> How is it limited? Why does she call for black women to make films?

Simmonds argues that, because the film is so very much the product of a black person (Lee directed it, wrote it, edited it and plays one of Nola's three lovers), the statements it makes about black female sexuality will be taken more seriously, indeed seen as 'truth'. They are, however, the statements of a black man, and women inside the film and outside it are silenced. It defines women and their aspirations in terms of sexuality, ignoring political and economic aspects. Simmonds argues that black women's film making is required to avoid the new images of black women being merely non-racist versions of those previously operating.

You may have been aware, in looking at the still, or in thinking about the film, that this image of a woman was removed from you in many ways – by being American if you are British, by being black if you are white, by being hetereosexual if you are lesbian, by being young if you are old – or you may have felt closer because of shared characteristics. When we feel close to, or identify with a character, it is usually because of some shared characteristic – maybe in this case a shared femaleness, or perhaps a desire not to have to settle for just one lover. This is itself a negotiation of our reading of the film and we must be aware that it can lead us to underplay some aspects of the film's meaning. For many of us, feeling close to Nola as a woman, may involve ignoring her distinctiveness as a black woman.

ARTICLE 4.3 'A WOMAN'S SPACE: WOMEN AND SOAP OPERA' BY CHRISTINE GERAGHTY

> Read now the opening paragraph and the first major section, 'The Personal Sphere', of Article 4.3 (pp. 221–231).

Christine Geraghty uses a similar distinction to that advanced by Gledhill, separating the social subject from the subject positions constructed by the text. She also suggests a further distinction by referring to the 'responses of individual viewers' (p. 221).

> What extra dimensions does this allow her to refer to? Why does she say that soaps may be seen as unmanly?

In referring to individual viewers, Geraghty comments on the way some viewers enjoy the spectacle but not the emotional demands of *Dallas*, for example. This warns us against developing a mechanistic idea of audience response determined by demographics – the kind of approach that might say that a white middle-class forty-something lesbian would be sure to make this kind of meaning from this collection of images.

CHAPTER 4 NEGOTIATING MEANINGS FROM POPULAR TELEVISION AND FILM

To my mind, the most important reasons Geraghty advances for soaps being seen as unmanly is that women, their activities and concerns are seen as more important than men and their activities and concerns, and that while it is important that female characters' actions are comprehensible to other female characters and to the female audience, male characters (and, perhaps by implication, male viewers) can be left uncomprehending.

► **ACTIVITY 39** ◄

Geraghty presents the views of two critics of soap opera and its viewers, the American critic Tania Modleski and the British critic Charlotte Brunsdon. List the main points of each and note why Geraghty prefers Brunsdon's perceptions.

COMMENT

Modleski sees soaps mirroring housewives' fragmented and distracted days and valuing the tolerance of the understanding mother. Brunsdon, on the other hand, argues that they require an audience with competence not only in reading the soap genre and the specific soap itself but also in knowing and operating the moral and ideological frameworks by which personal life is conducted. Geraghty prefers Brunsdon's presentation of a female audience with skills, rather than Modleski's, which she describes as being that of a masochistic and powerless viewer (p. 226).

Now read the rest of the article dealing with the other part of the duality – the public sphere (pp. 231–236).

► **ACTIVITY 40** ◄

How does Geraghty suggest that soaps present the interaction of public and private spheres? List the various critical charges about the way in which soaps present the public world of work and politics. How does Geraghty respond to these charges?

COMMENT

Geraghty sees the choice and representation of businesses and work locations being determined by the continuing primacy of personal and emotional concerns, so family businesses and work places where gossip can continue are more likely than the impersonal or noisy places that may be more common in 'real life'. Private and public lives are rarely successfully kept separate and external power relationships usually ignored. Geraghty acknowledges that in this way soaps attempt to explain economic affairs in the personal terms in which the audience is deemed to be competent and is thus incapable of addressing the complexities of contemporary capitalism. She argues, however, that there are positive aspects to this in that more economically self-sufficient women are shown than is usually the case.

Soaps provide particular pleasures not just to female viewers but also, as is particularly evident from the audiences for Australian soaps in the UK, for the young. It may be that there is something more complex than a gender distinctiveness in the audiences for soap – an interaction with age and possibly even social class. There are a considerable number of studies of soap opera audiences which address questions about the ways in which audiences choose, use and enjoy the programmes. The following are excerpts from interviews conducted as part of some of these studies.

1 An Australian teenage fan of *Coronation Street,* interviewed by Mary Ellen Brown:

> E: ... You'd be talking about things in general and you'd suddenly throw in a line from Mavis.
>
> ME: A real line that she had said? Or one that ...
>
> E: You'd say something in a Mavis voice. I mean there's great lines from Bet Lynch that you ... things like put-downs mainly, mainly probably put-downs to men which is why she is popular in her role as a barmaid, how she puts people down. Because I don't know whether you've seen it, but there was this barman Fred Gee, a great big fat obnoxious bloke, who really fancies himself – you know what fancies himself means? I don't know whether it means the same thing in America.
>
> ME: He was full of himself.
>
> E: Really fancies himself, thinks he's a real hit with the women, but isn't actually and is extremely unpleasant and obnoxious generally. Most women find him that, and he would always get into situations when he would dress up and put on aftershave and perhaps a cravat and look absolutely ridiculous and then he would try and get off with someone.
>
> ME: And then Bet would come in?
>
> E: And he'd be preening himself in front of the mirror very pleased with himself and he'd say, 'How do I look then, Lynch?' and she'd say, 'Oh, you look like a well-scrubbed pig.' So you'd use that line – or you'd just really appreciate that line.
>
> ME: So, it becomes almost like a code, that only the readers could ...
>
> E: If somebody was in the bar, Bet Lynch would say something to someone and they would be shocked and they'd have their mouth open, and she'd say something like, 'Shut your mouth before I drive a bus into it'.
>
> (M.E. Brown, recorded interview, September 1986, from Brown, 1990, pp. 193–4)

2   A 20-year-old British woman talking about the way the women she works with in a telephone sales office talk about soaps, interviewed by Dorothy Hobson:

> Well, it would be quite funny actually, what would happen would be somebody would talk about something that had happened in a program. The hypothetical situation that they might be in is that their husband had been unfaithful and they found out. And they would be coming out with this and that of what they would do. 'Well, I'd pack his bags, send him off, put him outside, wouldn't have him back!' And there would be all this big palaver going on. And then you would have people who it had actually happened to or it was happening to and they would begin to talk in the abstract, as in, 'But what if you loved him? But what if he said?' They would try to get the reactions from the other girls. I suppose it was a way to assess their own feelings and situations.

(Quoted in Hobson, 1990, p. 65)

3   Older people are a (critically) neglected section of the audience, but John Tulloch has published a small study of elderly soap opera viewers, from which I have taken the following comments of a Bournemouth pensioner:

> Really, I build my life around television ... *Dallas* is really soapbox ... all wonderful dresses and glamorous girls. Believe me, I like *Dallas* ... and *Dynasty* ... But I prefer the Australian ones ... I wouldn't miss *Sons and Daughters* if I could help it, because the story holds me. It always ends on a note that you are wondering where the next programme's going ... That makes a person want to switch it on. *A Country Practice* I like very much ... It's just sort of natural, down-to-earth everyday life ... and its scenery is nice ... And there's no swearing ... It's clean. There is no rape or anything. I think that's refreshing ... I don't like *EastEnders* because it's so down to earth ... Life is very drab, anyway for me ... People listening, like myself, like to be uplifted a bit.

(Quoted in Tulloch, 1990, p. 210)

How do these pieces of evidence exemplify, expand and contradict Geraghty's article?

The three examples seem to indicate that what is taken from soap operas and the way audiences use them may vary with age (though the sample is far too small to be the basis of any definite claims). For the Australian teenager, a soap character can provide an example of a useful linguistic style – something that might help her directly in her own personal interactions. The young British woman, talking about her fellow workers, notes how the personal competencies Brunsdon identified are exercised through the exploration of possible 'fits' between the fictions and various viewers' private lives. For the older viewer, there is much more disjunction between 'real life' and programme material. The favoured programmes appear to be those that depict a different world, one where things are more glamorous, or nicer and uplifting.

ARTICLE 4.4 'CONFESSION TIME: WOMEN AND GAME SHOWS'[6] BY FRANCES BONNER

Now read Article 4.4 (pp. 237–246), concentrating first on the distinction between 'ordinary' and 'extraordinary' people. What is this distinction based on?

'Extraordinary' people are generally given more time and the hosts control activities. Although Bonner does not say so in the article, an imbalance of knowledge is also relevant; viewers generally know far more about the 'extraordinary' people than is revealed during the programme – they are the subjects of newspaper and magazine stories or appear on radio and television chat shows, for example. 'Ordinary' people, on the other hand, only appear on the programmes and can only represent themselves there in terms of what the host and the programme allow. 'Ordinariness' rests substantially on being placed as a member of a family group.

Bonner pays particular attention in the article to the moment at which the contestants are introduced, arguing that this provides the viewer with the basic information on which to assess ordinariness and from which to draw points of identification or loyalty.

Why does she suggest that sexuality is so frequently the focus of host–contestant conversation?

Following Michel Foucault's arguments about the importance of the confession in the production of 'truth' in contemporary societies, Bonner sees the introductory chats and, where they exist, later interactions as providing the viewing audience with data about how other ordinary people 'truly' are. Focusing this on sexuality, and relating the family to this by, for example, focusing on the honeymoon or, as in the case of dating games, structuring the whole show around sexuality, is another instance of the prime place of sex as the 'defining quality of the self', to quote Simmonds in Article 4.2 (p. 220).

► **ACTIVITY 41** ◄

The section of dialogue from *Blind Date*, reproduced below, is an extension of the segment in Bonner's article. Read it now and make a note of your responses to the following questions:

(a) What precise 'confessions' is Cilla Black requiring from the guests?

(b) What presuppositions does the transcript reveal about dating and marriage?

> *(Rachel and Chris went on a weekend date to Paris. Part of the date involved catwalk modelling at a fashion show and culminated in their modelling wedding clothing. They are reporting back.)*
>
> *Cilla:* You did say at the top of the film there, Chris, that you didn't want to make the first move, you are not that type of person.
>
> *Chris:* Yes, well I didn't realize that I hadn't made the first move until I got home, we went back to see my family and my wee cousin said 'oh she's lovely, did you kiss her?' and I thought about it and I thought I knew there was something I'd forgotten.
>
> […]

---

[6] John Tulloch's work, quoted above, on the older audience, also includes references to his interviewees' comments on their enjoyment of game shows.

Cilla: And that wedding dress was super and you said, you sort of put yourself down there, that probably that would be the only wedding dress you'd ever wear.

Rachel: Probably.

Chris: She looked absolutely gorgeous. Honest, I felt like getting the vicar in then and there.

[...]

Cilla: Then the burning question. Is she ever going to get to wear that superb wedding dress, Chris?

Chris: I reckon she should. She looked so good in it. I reckon when she does, she ought to call them over in Paris and say send it over. And I felt so good standing beside her, even though I felt like the pageboy; but no, she looked so good that I would consider it an honour to be standing next to her, the way she looked then.

Rachel: Thank you, Chris. [Kiss.]

Cilla: Ooh, look at that. Well I think you make a super couple and if anything does develop, you know, let us know 'cos we'll get that wedding frock for you.

Rachel: Would you really?

Cilla: Oh yes. But you've got to marry him, though. Only on condition you marry him, because you do make a super, very attractive, couple. Don't they ladies and gentlemen? [Audience agrees.] Even your names go together. A lorra lorra luck to the both of you.

(Transcription from ITV Blind Date, transmitted on 25 January 1991)

COMMENT

The chosen segments focus on transition: the first kiss which marks the initial move to a (potentially) sexual relationship; the man's recognition that the woman is a possible wife; and Cilla's attempt to push matters forward. There are, however, other points to notice: that male sexual reticence must be commented on; that a woman's saying she did not expect to get married is a comment on her attractiveness or confidence rather than on her view of the institution; and perhaps even the economic component – the 'bribe' of the dress offer. It is also worth pondering on the importance of the visual – though since *Blind Date* is a television programme this is inevitable – the desirability and compatability of the couple are registered in the way they are said to look.

ACTIVITY 42

I would like you to conduct your own analysis of a game show. If access to a television set is difficult, an alternative using radio will be given after these directions, but this is less satisfactory because radio game shows and quizzes are quite different. You should choose a thirty-minute prime-time game show which does not use celebrity guests but which includes a segment where the host (female or male) asks contestants about themselves. Good examples from the time at which I am writing this would be *Strike It Lucky*, *Every Second Counts*, *Bull's Eye* or *Bruce Forsyth's Generation Game*. Shows like *Mastermind*, *Fifteen-to-One* or *The Krypton Factor* are not recommended because the hosts spend little or no time chatting to the contestants.

Your analysis should concentrate on this chat, but you should not neglect the rest of the programme. The purpose of your study is to investigate the way in which gender is presented and discussed in the programme. Start by examining the people who appear and what you are told about them. Does the host have an initial chat to the audience or to another host before the introduction of the contestants? If so, what is it about? How does she or he address other people (if the host is a man, does he call women 'dear'? Does anyone get called 'Mrs' or 'Mr'?)? What kind of contestant comments are elaborated on?

You should pay less attention to the questions and the prizes, but these can still be surprisingly gendered or family directed (prizes may include 'his-n-hers bathrobes' or 'a swing for the kiddies', or a game may be regarded as amusing or difficult because it cuts across gender expectations – a man icing a cake, for example).

COMMENT

Game shows are continually modified, unsuccessful formats dropped and new ones introduced. It is likely that some of the programmes referred to in the article will have disappeared, descriptive details will have changed and new types gained prominence. This makes it difficult to comment on what you may have found. It would be cheering to think that the shows you have been analysing will not carry the signs of gender expectations as strongly as did those prevalent at the time the article was written.

Radio alternative: most game and quiz shows on radio are either celebrity shows or are intellectual quizzes like *Brain of Britain*, neither of which are concerned to allow 'ordinary' people to represent themselves. This does not mean that there is no place of 'ordinariness' on radio. It is instead shown in phone-ins and talk-back programmes. Try to find a local programme of this kind and analyse the way it presents 'ordinariness' and gender-specific assumptions in terms as similar as possible to those you have been directed to for television game shows.

6
CHAPTER 5
PORNOGRAPHY AND REPRESENTATION
(FIRST HALF OF WEEK 30)
(prepared by Lizbeth Goodman)

Your work in the half week allotted to this part of the course will be organized around your reading of Chapter 5 of *Imagining Women*. This chapter focuses on pornography as a form of representation which is relevant to women's studies in two distinct ways: (1) because women are often depicted as bodies and body parts rather than as 'whole people'; and (2) because the subject of pornography has initiated so much debate within feminist activism and theory.

Chapter 5 comprises six readings: an introduction and five short articles. Because this is a fair amount of reading for half a week, the Study Guide for this part has been designed to help you understand and analyse the issues raised in these articles, rather than to approach the issues and extend them into more detailed discussions. You will be asked to read the introduction and five articles in order, keeping certain questions in mind as you read. First, it is important to consider the place of pornography, as a subject, in an academic course on issues in women's studies.

Because pornography is a contentious political subject, we hope you will see that it is also an appropriate and necessary subject for academic study. In particular, we hope that the connection between the forms of representation you have encountered in previous parts of *Imagining Women* will inform your study of pornography as another form of representation. Some of the themes you encountered in Chapter 4, for instance, are also relevant here: the study of the gendered gaze and of different ways of looking at images; questions of power and control over the production of visual images; questions of power and control over the viewing of images; and of course, the central question of women's role(s) in various forms of cultural representation.

In Chapters 3 and 4, you were encouraged to think of visual representations in women's art work and media images of women in terms of the renegotiation of meanings, depending on the viewpoints of different spectators in different cultural contexts. Similarly, pornography can be studied as a form of cultural representation which intersects in complicated ways with the representation of women in terms of gender, race, class, age and power relations in society. Like most of the forms of cultural representations we have examined in this course, pornography is seen and interpreted differently according to the viewpoints of the creators and spectators of the images.

Because pornographic images of various kinds have become so visible in the modern world, the debate around the subject of pornography has extended from one of moral or ethical issues into larger debates involving questions of obscenity and censorship. These debates are not divided so much by gender as by political perspective. In other words, we will not be looking in this section at differences between women's and men's approaches to the pornography debate, but rather at differences of perspective within feminist thought. Several different feminist perspectives are represented in the articles you are about to read.

CHAPTER 5 INTRODUCTION

Begin by reading the introduction to Chapter 5 (pp. 247–249).

CHAPTER 5 PORNOGRAPHY AND REPRESENTATION

The introduction is quite brief and functions as an outline of the ideas to be raised in the articles which follow. This introduction, and indeed all the articles in Chapter 5, deal with two key issues: the distinction between 'pornography' and 'erotica' and the issue of censorship. The latter is more directly confronted in the articles themselves. The former, however, is often assumed in the way different authors use the term 'pornography'. It may therefore be helpful to do an activity which engages with this important distinction, before moving on to read the articles.

▶ **ACTIVITY 43** ◀

Take out your dictionary and look up the terms 'pornography' and 'erotica'. Write down the definitions you find, and think about the distinction between the two terms. Do these definitions match your experience of the way the terms are used in everyday life?

Many people find that dictionary definitions of 'pornography' and 'erotica' are not the same as the operative definitions used in social interaction. In the most general sense, the term 'pornography' is often used to refer to a range of images, primarily of women's naked or semi-clad bodies. Images which depict women (and sometimes children) in ways which suggest violence against them are also generally called 'pornographic'. The related idea that pornographic images may actually incite violence against women is also a common cause for concern, and one which is discussed in several of the articles in this chapter.

The term 'erotica' is rarely used in daily conversation: it is a more specialized word, related to the concept of 'the erotic', which tends to be used in connection with 'desire' or with sensual suggestiveness rather than sexual explicitness. You may well have different commonsense definitions of these two terms, and different experiences of their common usage.

However you might define these two terms, it is unlikely that your definitions precisely match those you found in your dictionary. The *Oxford English Dictionary* reveals that 'pornography' was first used as a term for the 'representation of whores', while 'erotica' derives from the word 'eros': related to ancient ideas about 'sensual/sensuous' love. Definitions of the term 'pornography' shifted in the late seventeenth and early eighteenth centuries when 'obscenity' was introduced as a quality to be censored in various forms of (what we now call) cultural representations. Modern usage of the term is very different: it tends to refer to sexually explicit imagery, and is rarely concerned with prostitutes (as living people) or with literature (the most common medium for the 'obscene' in the eighteenth century). In 1927, 'obscene libel' was introduced into British common law as an offence (it must be remembered that all the definitions discussed here originate in the English language and in the cultural context of the UK, extended to other cultures through adaptation of the *Oxford English Dictionary* into other cultures).

The definition of the word 'erotica' is also culturally and temporally specific. Ancient Greek ideas about sensual/sensuous love seem quite hazy and romantic, while the word 'erotica' for us today may not have anything to do with 'love' but rather with desire. The distinction between pornography and erotica is one of the most contentious issues in contemporary discussions of pornography and representation.

The distinction between 'pornography' and 'erotica' is explored in the last article in Chapter 5. It is also raised indirectly in all the articles, in the sense that a distinction between the two terms has implications for discussion of the censorship issue. Some argue, for instance, that the blurred distinction between pornography and erotica renders it impossible to allow for the censorship of one (pornography) without the censorship of the other (erotica), while others argue that the distinction between the two is what makes it possible to advocate censorship of pornography. Opponents of censorship may dislike pornography, but believe that there is a positive place for erotica in women's lives, that women's general investigation of their own sexualities would be curbed by imposing limitations on the right to representation and expression. Thus, it is possible to defend the concept of women's right to self-expression both from an anti-pornography and an anti-censorship standpoint.

In discussing the distinction between pornography and erotica, the censorship question has already emerged. This overlap in discussion of two important aspects of the pornography debate illustrates the intricate connection between the issues. In fact, much debate has focused on the question of whether it is possible to separate the issue of defining pornography from the issue of censorship.

ARTICLE 5.1 *'LACE:* PORNOGRAPHY FOR WOMEN?' BY AVIS LEWALLEN

You should read Article 5.1 now (pp. 250–257), asking yourself the following questions as you do so:
How does Lewallen implicitly define pornography?
Does she advocate or oppose censorship of pornographic images?

Lewallen's definition of pornography is quite wide – it includes images of women in popular fiction and the media, as well as those images more commonly associated with the term 'pornography'. Lewallen uses the term 'soft porn' to refer to sexually explicit images of a certain kind: those sometimes found in blockbuster novels as well as in other widely distributed forms such as advertisements, 'Page Three' and so forth. (The other authors in this part do not use the terms 'soft porn' or 'hard porn', perhaps because the definitions of these terms are so highly subjective.) Lewallen looks to blockbuster novels written by women, which depict what she calls 'soft porn', in order to explore the expression of female sexuality in the representation of women by women. She asks questions about the representation of women in 'pornographic' literature which are very similar to the questions asked about the representation of women in visual media: 'If these texts can be classified as "soft porn", what position is being offered to the female reader? Do they merely contribute to the further objectification of women within our misogynist society, inculcating male power, or do they offer a form of representation that facilitates the female gaze?' (p. 250). The emphasis on the reader's response will be familiar to you as a feminist concern in studies of representation, from your work on Chapters 3 and 4; the reader takes the same position as the viewer or spectator of visual images, including pornographic images.

You may also find echoes of arguments from other chapters of *Imagining Women*. For instance, the blockbuster novel (*Lace*), which Lewallen discusses in terms of its pornographic depiction of women, might have been included as an example of the kind of novel found in supermarket sale bins, in your response to Activity 17, when you were working on Article 2.2. In that article, the idea of 'supply and demand' was approached in terms of the lasting quality of stereotyped images of women, in the context of a larger discussion of genres and ways of expressing feminist politics in fiction.

Lewallen takes a similar approach to a different subject. She argues that fictions such as *Lace* may be partially liberating for women, in their depiction of women actively seeking and gaining sexual pleasure. She sees *Lace* as a novel in which heterosexual women are empowered through their active initiation of and dominance in sexual activity. Lewallen sees this development as a result of women's writing of these blockbusters, once the influence of feminism made it easier for women to gain recognition as writers. She argues that the writing of such 'soft porn' novels need not be seen as negative, but may be viewed as a positive achievement for both feminism and for the mass market. In this sense, Lewallen invokes a version of the 'supply and demand' argument when she discusses the implications of mass market availability of pornographic images in 'literature' which is not often labelled 'pornography'.

In this regard, it is interesting to note that the rise of the English novel in the eighteenth and nineteenth centuries roughly coincided with the introduction of 'obscenity' as a quality to be censored in literary representations. Even in the eighteenth century, a distinction was made between some literature – for instance, Samuel Richardson's *Clarissa* – and less literary novels depicting sex – such as the infamous *Fanny Hill*, published and banned concurrently with the publication of *Clarissa*. Such distinctions between 'high art' and 'popular culture' or 'folk art' still operate in modern societies, and pornographic images in higher status media ('arty' films and photographs, for instance) are often assumed to have more 'artistic' value and cultural validity than, for instance, 'lower' forms such as pornographic videos and magazines. Yet, as in Lewallen's use of the term 'soft porn', the identification of 'degrees' of pornography, or of forms of media in which pornographic imagery may be more acceptable (in *Clarissa* or *Lady Chatterley's Lover* rather than in *Penthouse*) is very problematic indeed.

Lewallen's article contributes two valuable points to this discussion of pornography and representation: her observations about the market appeal of pornographic fiction, and about the relevance of both reader reception and the gender of the writer. Her view that the representations offered in 'soft porn' fiction may be empowering for women is more contentious. Lewallen proposes that there could be a women's pornography if power relations in society were more equal. Is this proposition overly optimistic? In the present social state of gendered power relations the concept of 'women's pornography' is potentially problematic. Keep this in mind as you read the next article.

ARTICLE 5.2 'OBSCENITY AND CENSORSHIP' BY SUZANNE KAPPELER

Please now read Article 5.2 (pp. 258–262), bearing the following questions in mind:
How does Kappeler define 'pornography'?
How does she deal with the issue of censorship?

Suzanne Kappeler defines pornography as a system of representation which depends upon the unequal distribution of power in relation to gender. She argues that it is crucial that women recognize the ways in which verbal and visual representations perpetuate and express the victimization of subordinate groups in unequal societies. Kappeler uses the term 'the pornography of representation' to refer to the ways in which certain kinds of representations can be used in order to keep some people in positions of power over others, primarily – in western societies – men in control over women, or over images of women.

Kappeler argues that pornography exists in and contributes to the sustaining of unequal societies. She suggests that the term 'pornography' is inadequate to describe the potential for such representations to demean the people they objectify, and to maintain and support unequal power structures in society (demonstrated by the gendered division between those who usually make pornographic images, and those who are usually depicted in them).

The differences in levels of power between those who control the means of production of pornographic images and those who are depicted in them is often reflected in the images themselves – for instance, in images of women in subordinate positions depicted for the consumption of a 'male gaze'. When the factor of race is added to the analysis of pornography in terms of gender, the issue of power becomes even more compelling. This point is developed in the next article, which can be usefully read in conjunction with the Kappeler article.

ARTICLE 5.3 'PORNOGRAPHY AND BLACK WOMEN'S BODIES' BY PATRICIA HILL COLLINS

Now read Article 5.3 (pp. 263–267) and, as you do so, pay particular attention to the parallel which Hill Collins describes between the treatment of black slave women by white masters (in the past) and the ways in which black women are treated in representational terms by (mostly white male) creators of pornographic images today.

Patricia Hill Collins argues that in pornographic images today, as in the real situation of slavery in the past, women are represented as objects. She draws a parallel between the treatment of women and the treatment of animals, arguing that the subordinate and submissive positioning of both is typical of certain power relationships in society, as represented in pornography. Hill Collins argues that the genealogy of modern pornography can be traced in the iconography of the nineteenth century. She gives the example of black slaves who were exhibited naked, displaying their genitals (as are women in pornographic images today). As in pornography, Hill Collins argues, so it was the case in the public display of black women's bodies in the slave trade, that the personhood and dignity of the individual woman was (is) erased in her depiction as a sexual body.

By approaching the subject of pornography in terms of race/gender analysis, Hill Collins emphasizes the ways in which black and white women may see their images intertwined in the iconography of masculine domination. The article points out that racism has been instrumental in representation, a view that can be supported with reference to images which depict black women as sexual slaves and white women as Madonnas. Here, you may recall the discussion in Chapter 2 of the over-simplistic dichotomies (angel, whore etc.) often employed in constructing stereotyped images of women. This same kind of dichotomy is analysed by Michelle Cliff in her discussion of visual images in Article 3.2, while the image of the black woman as a sexual being on film is analysed in Article 4.2. Thus, Hill Collins' arguments about the depiction of black women's bodies in pornography can be usefully contrasted with several other articles in *Imagining Women*.

This article does not argue either for or against censorship, nor does it explicitly define either 'pornography' or 'erotica'. Instead, the article argues from the perspective of a black woman who sees important historical and cultural parallels in the treatment of black women in society, and of black (and white) women in pornography. Hill Collins cites the historical representation of black women as slaves and sexual beings to support the idea that there is a relationship between the way women are represented and viewed, and the way women are treated in society.

You may or may not agree with this analysis. In either case, it is important to take account of its implications by asking whether the representation of black women's bodies is a special case, or one example of a larger problem. Can we extend the arguments put by Hill Collins to say that the representation of women's bodies in pornography has real effects on the way women are treated? Can we prove it? This is, of course, one of the most important and difficult issues raised by feminist debates about pornography. Different ways of approaching this question are addressed in the next two articles, both of which explore the distinction between real and represented violence against women in relation to the debate concerning the censorship of pornography.

ARTICLE 5.4 'WHO WATCHES THE WATCHWOMEN?: FEMINISTS AGAINST CENSORSHIP' BY GILLIAN RODGERSON AND LINDA SEMPLE

Please now read Article 5.4 (pp. 268–273).

► **ACTIVITY 44** ◄

As you read this article, make a list of the arguments offered in support of the anti-censorship position of the authors.

COMMENT

In this article, the authors offer a variety of arguments in support of the anti-censorship position. Here is a list of some of these (paraphrased) arguments:

1   There is no proven relationship between actual and represented violence against women.
2   Censorship would harm freedom of speech and expression.
3   The way to counter sexist images is to create images of alternative kinds (positive images of women).
4   There should be open and safe communication about sex, including its power relations and including freedom of expression of lesbian and gay sexualities.

Two of these arguments are particularly relevant to those put forward in the previous articles. The argument that there is no proven relationship between actual and represented violence against women undercuts the idea – extrapolated from the previous article by Patricia Hill Collins – that the historical representation of black women's bodies (in the slave trade) informs and may have influenced the current representation of women's bodies in pornography. But the two arguments are not mutually exclusive. Rodgerson and Semple do not dismiss the idea that pornography represents violence against women (as Hill Collins argued with her example of black women in chains in the slave trade). Nor do they argue that there is no relationship between actual and represented violence. Rather, Rodgerson and Semple argue that such a relationship has not been proved.

The question of whether such a relationship does exist, and if so, whether it could ever be 'proved' to exist, is very complicated. Some have argued that there may be a relationship between pornography and real violence, citing rape and domestic violence as examples of represented violence influencing real violence against women in society (one example of this kind of argument is included in the reference to 'Ms U's story' in the next article). Many disagree vehemently. But even those who agree in principle find difficulty in 'proving' a relationship between represented and actual violence against women. The dilemma is worth considering quite carefully, as it lies at the heart of the pornography and censorship debate. The following activity has been designed to help you to see some of the different sides of this question.

▶ **ACTIVITY 45** ◀

Look at the arguments in the extract below, taken from the Feminists Against Censorship leaflet, Summer 1989. (The title page of this leaflet appears on page 273 of Book Four.) List the three main points raised in this material, and ask yourself whether any of these points actually contradicts what has been said in the previous articles.

Who defines pornography?

Much commercially available pornography is racist and misogynist. In a racist, misogynist society this is no surprise. It is possible to criticize specific pieces of pornography without being in favour of increasing the State's power to suppress pornography itself and without regarding sexually explicit material as bad in itself.

Even those who agree that sexually explicit material should be suppressed find it impossible to agree on what should go. The traditional pro-censorship lobby would destroy lesbian and gay material in the name of the Family. They seek to suppress safer sex information on the grounds that it encourages homosexuality. They have done everything in their power to prevent distribution of information about birth control and abortion: they consider this to be pornography as well. There is also sincere disagreement among anti-pornography feminists. Some argue that nudity alone is pornographic, others that the problem is violent pornography alone. With this much disagreement even among feminists, who can you trust? Do you think the Government will appoint feminists as censors?

Instead of striking a blow against women's oppression, censorship gives the patriarchy additional ammunition. It is inconsistent to oppose Clause 28 one year and support censorship the next.

Pornography, a red herring?

In the words of the Campaign Against Pornography (CAP), "Pornography ... violates women's rights to safety and equality, encourages and legitimates the abuse of women and children, sexually and emotionally, and involves the abuse and exploitation of women and children in its production."

Strong stuff, but women's oppression in society is more complex than this.

Let's talk about real violence against women, not just images. Violence has multiple causes, one of which may be a high consumption of violent images. Studies are inconclusive. Most suggest violent images have no impact and that it makes no difference whether the images are sexually explicit. Yet it is precisely the comparatively rare combination of violent and sexually explicit images in pornography that anti-pornography feminists see as being at the root of women's oppression in society. Why are they ignoring the fundamental causes of cultural and social oppression? Their single minded focus on pornography has distracted attention from more effective feminist responses to violence and oppression; for example women's refuges, self-defence initiatives, alternative media, campaigns for better transport and better sex education, and attempts to make women economically independent.

Is pornography really the problem? Is its suppression really going to change women's low economic status? Will it remove the real violence which sustains unequal power? Many anti-pornography feminists are so concerned with pornography that they are ignoring the damage done to women by cuts in the NHS, the increase in racist attacks, assaults on lesbians and gay men, the promotion by the government of an ideology which reduces the freedom of women in the name of the Family and the erosion of women's rights throughout the world.

Censorship is dangerous

Anti-pornography feminists' solution to male violence is a dangerous new departure. The belief that there are direct causal links between pornography and violence has led groups like CAP to advocate authoritarian measures. These include censorship, euphemistically referred to as 'legislation against pornography'. The danger allegedly posed by pornography is said to justify increasing the power of the State and trusting it not to abuse that power.

(From: Feminists Against Censorship leaflet 'Ask yourself ... do you really want more censorship?', Summer 1989)

COMMENT

The three main points raised in this extract are:

1. The section headed 'Who defines pornography?' points to the racist and misogynist bias of most commercially available pornographic materials, and of those in positions of power who might decide what 'pornography' is and which materials and images should be censored. This argument reminds us that race is at issue as well as gender and power (as Hill Collins argued); it also emphasizes a need to recognize the diversity of opinion, even among feminists, as to what 'pornography' is.

2. The second section is headed: 'Pornography, a red herring?'. This section acknowledges that pornographic images often depict violence against women, and that there may be some connection between these images and

real violence. Yet the authors argue that it is too simplistic to cite pornography as the root of all violence against women. The authors do not suggest that there is no connection, but rather that the connection should not be overstated; that the focus of feminist thought should – more practically – be on women's status (real and representational) in all areas of society, all over the world.

3   The third section has the self-explanatory title: 'Censorship is dangerous'. In this section, the authors reiterate their belief that censorship is not the way to improve women's status in society, nor to protect women from violence (real or representational).

These same issues are addressed, in the context of the other articles in this section as well as in larger terms, in the fifth and last article in Chapter 5.

ARTICLE 5.5 'THE PORNOGRAPHY PROBLEM' BY LIZBETH GOODMAN

Read Article 5.5 now (pp. 274–283). It will be most helpful if you read this article as a kind of response to the general issues raised in the pornography debate, rather than as a response to the previous articles (remembering that there are many other perspectives which might also be represented).

As this article was written specifically for publication in *Imagining Women*, it can be most directly and fairly analysed in terms of its place in your studies in this course. The article contextualizes some of the most contentious issues raised in the analysis of pornography, and suggests that these might best be viewed as points along a continuum.

For instance, Goodman argues that the views of Feminists Against Censorship and those who advocate censorship should not be seen as mutually exclusive or diametrically opposed, but rather as different perspectives on the same problem, or different positions on a continuum of feminist thought. Many who are opposed to pornography in most of its more extreme forms (hardcore pornographic images and films etc.) may be more tolerant of 'softer' images, or of the kind of pornography which Avis Lewallen describes in popular mass-marketed romances. More importantly, many who are opposed to pornography are also opposed to censorship. And of those who advocate censorship, there are degrees of censorship which are seen as desirable and degrees of censorship which are seen as undesirable, or even dangerous. Even those who oppose censorship occupy a number of different positions along the continuum of feminist thought.

Another issue which can be viewed in terms of a continuum is the distinction between 'pornography' and 'erotica'. The pornography/erotica distinction is discussed at length in Goodman's article. Most importantly, Goodman points out that the two terms are not defined in static objective ways. While the words – like all words – have etymological roots, they are used in various ways by different people, and their meanings have changed with different generations and social contexts. Thus, Goodman argues, the problem of pornography is not solely related to the pornographic images themselves, but also to the diversity of definitions and perspectives which the debate involves, the conditions of its production and consumption in society, its visibility to those who do not wish to see it, and most importantly, to the complex question of its legal status.

The question of censorship has a complex relationship with many different political perspectives. It also creates complicated interrelationships between one possible 'solution' (censorship or partial censorship of pornography) and a range of problems which such a 'solution' might create. Goodman argues that the problem of pornography is one of representation in a society which has rules and regulations encoded in both its laws and its common laws or precedents: rules about censorship and about the right to expression. Yet moral and ethical considerations also influence some people's views of pornography, and political positions such as feminism have influenced a growing awareness of the scale of the pornography industry.

Referring to pornography as a 'problem' may itself be problematic, in that it may imply a certain negativity, or emphasize the role of pornographic representations too strongly. Of course, feminists have focused on a very wide range of issues and debates, pornography being one example. But the issue of the status of women in society – as depicted in and perhaps influenced by images in the media, including pornographic images – is complicated by material circumstances; we live in a cultural context in which access to power is unevenly divided between women and men.

Some of the authors in Chapter 5 acknowledge the cultural impact of pornography in this era characterized by the rapid expansion of mass communication technologies. Some discuss this impact in terms of gender and class while others analyse it in terms of race. All of the authors emphasize the question of censorship, in one way or another. All express concern with the issue of women's status and with the representation of women in pornography and society.

CONCLUSION

In order to demonstrate that the issue of pornography and representation extends far beyond the bounds of 'pornography' as the term is commonly defined, I have provided an activity which deals with pornography in larger terms. Do this activity only if you have time before moving on to Chapter 6.

► **ACTIVITY 46** ◄

Look carefully at the image of Madonna in Figure 14, asking yourself the following questions:

(a) Is there something about Madonna's image which is deliberately provocative?

(b) Is it a positive or a negative image?

(c) Can such questions be answered with regard to what we have learned about pornography as a form of cultural representation?

COMMENT

This image of Madonna can hardly be called 'pornography': it is not meant to represent women in negative ways, but rather in empowering ways (and, in fact, an entire generation of young women identify with Madonna as a positive role model). Yet the image is not positive in most conventional ways. It depicts a sexual (perhaps sensual) woman who has constructed a marketable image of herself, based on but possibly subverting sexual stereotypes (the hair dyed blonde to look

Figure 14

Madonna in performance. Photograph: London Features International/Billy Bong

like Marilyn Monroe etc.). By wearing her underwear on the outside, Madonna insists that her audience see that which they might otherwise (according to what we have learned about the male gaze) try to see, or to detect underneath her other garments. Madonna takes away the power of audience voyeurism by showing her underwear as outerwear: by creating an image which is both sexual and asexual, depending upon our interpretations.

Madonna's image is one of the best known in contemporary western culture, and in many other cultures as well (as she has been very successfully 'sold' to countries around the world). Whether you like Madonna's music or not, whether you like her style or not, whether you are offended or amused by her, it is difficult to deny her status as a media superstar. Her notoriety has been enhanced by her self-styled defiant sexuality. She is notorious not only because of the sexually explicit lyrics of some of her songs and the 'bad girl' image she so powerfully projects, but also because she plays with religious and ethical conventions in her work. For instance, some of her songs parody the Catholic religion, and her music has been called 'sacrilegious'. One of her tour shows was banned as a result (though she performed the show, regardless). Banning her music seems to have operated as a guarantee to its popular success.

Similarly, in the USA in 1990, the Rap music of a male band called 2 Live Crew was banned on the basis of obscenity and oppressive representation of women. (The female rapper Queen Latifah, whose work is discussed in the next section of this Study Guide, writes music which empowers women, as a kind of antidote to the misogynist bias of much Rap music.) 2 Live Crew's second album, entitled 'Banned in the USA', was a top seller, despite the refusal of some record shops to stock it. Can this demonstration of the saleability of 'banned' images support some of the arguments of Feminists Against Censorship? Or is this a larger social phenomenon connected with ethical and religious issues and government and church powers over the media? Are the examples of sexually explicit and 'banned' images of Madonna and 2 Live Crew appropriate to the continuum idea?

You might want to discuss your response to these issues with friends, or with other students in tutorials.

There are no easy answers to questions such as those raised by this activity. It is, however, very important that these questions be posed and that you keep these issues and ideas in mind as you review the many different forms of cultural representations you have studied in the course. Some of these same issues will be raised in the next chapter of *Imagining Women*.

While discussion in the next chapter focuses on comedy as a feminist strategy, it brings in related issues such as the interpretation of cartoons depicting images of women. It also deals with the strategies of representation which women have employed in 'taking the mike' in stand-up comedy, writing feminist comedy for the theatre and singing about the power of women in Rap music. All of these cultural forms share a characteristic of pornography, in that all are about the representation of women. Yet while our discussion of pornography and representation has focused on issues of physical representation (the representation – largely by men – of bodies – mostly women's), the next part will look at the cultural representation of women in terms of a range of self-representations of and by women.

These two subjects, pornography and comedy, may seem very different. Yet you need not make too large a leap in terms of your own approach to their study, for the themes explored in both parts are very similar. Both parts are concerned with images or representations of women, and with the crucial issue of control over the means of production of those images.

7
CHAPTER 6 COMIC SUBVERSIONS (SECOND HALF OF WEEK 30)
(prepared by Lizbeth Goodman)

We have allowed half a week for this part of the course, in which your main task is to read Chapter 6 of *Imagining Women*. This part of the book is called 'Comic Subversions' and comprises three short pieces – an introduction and two readings: one on 'Gender and Humour' and one on 'Comedy as Strategy in Feminist Theatre'. You will be asked to read the conclusion to *Imagining Women* at the end of this week, before moving on to the final chapter of Book One *Knowing Women* in Week 31 and the Course Conclusion in Week 32.

In addition, two of the radio broadcasts have been designed to compliment the written material in Chapter 6: Radio Programme 10 *Agitfem: feminist theatre* and Radio Programme 11 *The Way She Tells 'Em: women comics*. You may also find that Television Programme 08 *Taking the Credit: women in TV* is particularly relevant to this part of the course.

BEGINNING YOUR STUDY OF COMIC SUBVERSIONS

The first thing you will notice when you read this part of the course is its relatively 'light' tone. There are a number of reasons for this. First, this part follows on from the study of pornography, and the stark contrast in theme from one half of the week to the next is purposefully designed to demonstrate that subjects which are similar in their shared concern with the representation of women may differ quite significantly in terms of their effects on women's lives. You may well have found the pornography material a bit difficult, in the sense that it is politically charged and perhaps also depressing. By contrast, you may – we hope – find the comedy material engaging, even entertaining. Yet both subjects are legitimate concerns in the study of representations of and by women.

There is not only one way of writing, or of reading, feminist material. By this point in the course, we hope that you are familiar enough with a range of different styles and approaches that this contrast between the serious and the comic will not jar, but rather will lead you to consider your own reactions to different kinds of arguments and topics.

Stop here and read the brief introduction to Chapter 6 (pp. 284–285).

► **ACTIVITY 47** ◄

Now review your notes from your reading of Chapter 5. You may notice that some of the themes which emerged in discussion of pornography and representation are repeated in the introduction to Chapter 6, where they are signalled as important themes for the book as a whole. List some of the common themes you find, even if they are worded slightly differently.

COMMENT

Your list might look something like this:

breaking the silence

breaking taboos

speaking out

subverting expectation and convention

representing women

putting self into performance (or into art work etc.)

In fact, these same ideas are raised throughout *Imagining Women*. In this sense, the themes and key ideas raised in this chapter are the same as those of the book as a whole. This is no accident. This material on comedy is not meant to introduce new ideas, but rather to present the central ideas of the fourth part of the course in more accessible ways. This use of comedy as a teaching tool at the end of the book is a subversive strategy in itself – we wanted to give you a break after a long six weeks of hard work, but also to encourage you to review the previous material and to re-view it by evaluating it in a more light-hearted way and in relation to your own life experiences.

With regard to the latter point, you will notice when you begin reading the two articles in Chapter 6 that both begin with quotations about the relationship between 'playing roles' and 'real life'. The first reading begins with a quotation from Roseanne Barr,[7] who compares her early experience of 'taking the mike' and taking on the persona of Roseanne the comedienne (on stage), arguing that it opened up a new way of seeing and dealing with her own life (off stage):

> One day, I read a quote: 'If a woman told the truth about her life, the world would split open.' I found a stage, where I began to tell the truth about my life – because I couldn't tell the truth off the stage. And very quickly, the world began to blow apart.
>
> (Barr, 1990, p. 202)

---

[7] Roseanne Barr has changed her name for personal/political reasons and is now known as Roseanne Arnold.

Figure 15
Cover of *Roseanne, My Life as a Woman* by Roseanne Barr, 1990

Similarly, the quotation which begins the second reading introduces the idea that women are expected to play many different roles in everyday life, all of which are defined in relation to expectations of gendered behaviour, and many of which may go against individual women's preferred forms of self-presentation or representation. This essay draws a comparison between women's role playing in everyday life and the role playing of the theatre. In feminist theatre – that is, theatre written by and arguably for women, with feminist intent – Goodman argues, the role playing associated with performance often overlaps with the role playing of everyday life, when feminist playwrights and performers subvert expectations about gendered behaviour in various ways. In feminist comic theatre, this subversion of expectation may be particularly effective because the comedy allows political statements to be swallowed (with a spoonful of sugar) and thereby renders the feminist politics palatable in a way which agit-prop and realist dramatic forms of representation do not.

Before reading these two essays, it is important to stop and consider what might be meant by the title of this part of *Imagining Women*: 'Comic Subversions'. It may help to analyse this idea in relation to a very accessible, popular form of comic representation: the cartoon.

CHAPTER 6 COMIC SUBVERSIONS

▶ **ACTIVITY 48** ◀

Look over the five cartoons below, and take note of your immediate responses (gut reactions) to them. Then look at them again, and ask yourself whether they have political messages which are conveyed particularly effectively through the medium of humour.

1

2

3

4

"What is GOOD feminist practice?"

5

"Why are VERY supportive enviroments VERY unsupported financially?"

1

2

3

4

5

COMMENT

The first cartoon – by a celebrated male cartoonist known for his political satires in mainstream newspapers – depicts Margaret Thatcher, the most celebrated 'housewife' appealing to her 'sister housewife' in order to gain her vote, and then making away with her riches (her promised reward, being the chance for upward mobility or improved social conditions and status for housewives). The message is clear: the cartoonist draws on the familiar story of Cinderella in order to suggest that Thatcher exploited her 'domestic' image in order to appeal to female voters, but was not concerned with women's status once she herself had gained a position of power in 'the palace'. The cartoon is composed of three boxed drawings or images, forming a sequence which, taken as a whole or 'read' from left to right, tell a story through pictures. In the first box, the expectation is set up; in the second, the promised reward materializes; and in the third, the comic subversion of expectation is represented (in the visual absence of Thatcher and her fancy car from the image, as she has clearly zoomed off to power).

This first cartoon can in no way be seen as a 'feminist strategy'. It is made by a man, and depicts a situation which undercuts the most basic ideas of feminism. But a similar strategy is used by feminist cartoonists such as Cath Jackson and Angela Martin in their cartoon illustrations for *Trouble and Strife* (a radical feminist journal) – see the next four cartoons. These do not need explication, their messages are clear. They take all the basic tenets of the women's movement and turn them on their heads, asking whether they might sometimes contradict the lived experience of individual women, even if they can be maintained as general rules or feminist principles. All four of these cartoons pose important political questions for feminism.

The second cartoon asks whether radical and socialist feminist politics may – in 1987 when the cartoons were published – have been challenging each other for the right to the title of 'proper feminism', thereby implying that these two schools of feminist thought are incompatible and that women supporting these schools might not be well suited to join together to fight for more general feminist principles such as 'A Woman's Right to Choose'. This cartoon does not contain a second 'boxed image', but if it did, it might be of a banner torn in half.

The absence of the second image is a feminist strategy in itself: it demands more work of the interpreters of the cartoon, who must decide for themselves where the situation depicted might lead. This cartoon might be seen as a light-hearted observation about the differences between feminist positions, or it might be seen more ominously as a warning: a danger to feminism if opposing camps cannot come to terms and hold the same big banners. The image need not be interpreted in one way to the exclusion of the other. Indeed, there are any number of possible interpretations of this image. The open image allows for interpretations of all kinds. This is part of its power, related to the power of the interpreting audience (an issue which is discussed in Article 6.2 about comic theatre, where the role of the audience is also crucial).

The images in the last three cartoons work in similar ways to make comic statements, but also to pose political questions for feminism. In all four of the feminist cartoons, the strategy of 'comic subversion' is used by the artists. It can also be used by the interpreters of the cartoons (you, the readers or 'audience' of the images) in the process of reviewing these images in terms of gender and cultural representations. With this in mind, the two articles in Chapter 6 can be seen to reflect the major concerns of the book in a very obvious, and hopefully entertaining, way.

The subject matter of both articles is similar, but not the same. The first deals with a variety of forms of comedy, including stand-up comedy and televised situation comedy, while the second deals with the theatrical comedy of the staged play.

CHAPTER 6 COMIC SUBVERSIONS

ARTICLE 6.1 'GENDER AND HUMOUR' BY LIZBETH GOODMAN

Please read Article 6.1 now (pp. 286–300), making a few notes about key themes and ideas as you do so.

The most common remark made by all the women interviewed, and quoted in this article, was that they felt a certain power – and a positive challenge – in standing up in front of a microphone to tell jokes. While women have often been 'featured' in comedy material by men, and have been the butt of jokes of different kinds, it is only recently that women have begun to tell their own jokes in public spaces. This position – of 'taking the mike', or assuming authority over the comic material – is a form of self-representation, and is still not always seen as 'acceptable' for women.

You may recall from your viewing of Television Programme 08 that women directors, producers, writers and editors are still relatively few. Women are more commonly thought of as performers, or 'actresses'. One way in which comedy can be informed by an awareness of gender difference – and indeed by a feminist perspective – is in its claiming of the means of communication (in this case, the joke or the comic sketch) in order to 'subvert' the norm by claiming the right of representation in this public forum.

In fact, the technician who did the recording on a few of the interviews for Radio Programme 11 (which you will soon listen to) was a man, but the questions were devised and asked by women (the producer and academic). Most importantly, of course, the comics are women. This would have been a very different study if we had interviewed male as well as female comics, or if we had sent a male interviewer to ask the questions (ours or his). Our interview technique was to invite the comedians to tell us what was most important to them: whether the work was feminist and subversive were put as open questions, and these terms were left for the comedians to define in the ways most relevant to their own experiences.

Figure 16
Spare Tyre (Harriet Powell and Clair Chapman).
Photograph: Ute Klaphake, courtesy of Spare Tyre Theatre Company

CHAPTER 6 COMIC SUBVERSIONS

Figure 17
Donna and Kebab (Eve Adams and Martha Lewis): poster for *Acropolis Now*, Assembly Hall, Edinburgh, August–September 1991. Photograph: Xenia Demetriou

Figure 18
Sheila Hyde. Photograph by courtesy of Equity

One of the main points we wanted to make with this material was that gender difference affects the way in which comics view themselves and their own roles as comics, or as creators of comic material. This perceived gender difference is clearly illustrated by Radio 11.

You might find it useful at this point to stop and read the Media Notes for the women comics radio programme. Use those notes in order to frame some ideas which will be made by the women interviewed in the programme itself (Helen Lederer, Spare Tyre, Lip Service, Sheila Hyde and Donna and Kebab). Many of them discuss their own physical appearance – what they wear when they perform, their body sizes, the importance of costumes – as well as the subject matter of their material. Some make jokes about making jokes, about the subjects which are considered 'acceptable' comic material: men's genitals but not women's periods etc.

Similar points could be made about women's making of music. An obvious parallel to the rise of women in comedy is the rise of women in popular music, and particularly in music associated with young audiences, such as Rock and Rap. 'Taking the mike' in making music is often associated with a direct assertion of authority over rhythm and style.

In Queen Latifah's Rap music, for instance, the emphasis is on women's right to 'take the mike' and to define the terms of their own music: its rhythm, its subject matter and its singers. The lyrics from one of Queen Latifah's best known songs are quite clearly subversive of mainstream cultural norms of women's silence, and quite comically so. An extract of this song, 'Ladies First', is reproduced here.

Ladies First (extract)

… Let me state the position: Ladies First
Yes? Yes!
(male voice: Yeah, there's gonna be some changes round here …)
Believe me when I say being a woman is great; you see
I know a lot of fellas out there will agree with me
not to being one, but to being with one
cause when it's time for lovin' it's the woman that gives 'em
strong steppin', struttin', movin' on, rhymin', cockin'
and not forgettin'
we're the ones that give birth
to a new generation of profits
cause it's Ladies First.
I break into a Liverpool free style
grab the mike; look at the crowd and see smiles
'cause they see a woman standin' up on her own two; sloppy slouchin' is somethin' I won't do
Some think that we can't flow (can't flow);
Stereotypes they got to go (got to go);
I'm gonna mess around and flip the scene into reverse …
(With what?)
With a little touch of Ladies First.

(Transcription from 'Ladies First', Queen Latifah All Hail the Queen, *1989, Tommy Boy Music Inc., New York. Also featuring Monie Love. Produced by D.J. Mark, the 45 King. Recorded at Studio 1212 and at Calliope Productions, New York*)

As Latifah and Monie Love sing later in the Rap, 'the title of this recital is Ladies First'. The song 'Ladies First' is an example of a woman's innovative strategy for breaking the silence and saying what is not normally said, and for using music and rhythm as well as comedy as means to her strategic end. It is interesting that Latifah, like most of the comediennes interviewed for Radio Programme 11, uses the phrase 'taking the mike' as a shorthand for taking the means of control of her own voice. The microphone is, of course, a powerful (phallic) symbol. Its ability to amplify voices and to make women heard in a literal sense has given it a symbolic as well as a real significance to women's work in many different fields, from entertainment to politics.

In interview, Queen Latifah is not only assertive but provocative. She uses her stage persona as 'Queen' to assert her right to make the kind of music she wants. Her chosen style of music is Rap: rhyming lyrics set to a beat, often improvised. Most Rap music has originated in the USA, and most has been made by black men, about (black) men's lives, often representing women in negative ways. Queen Latifah was one of the first women to break into Rap and to sing – or rap – about her own experience, about which she boldly asserts that she thinks her 'sisters, will agree with me'.

Some of the lyrics in 'Ladies First' challenge 'any man or wo-man, it makes no difference, keep the competition coming' to try to beat her at her own game: rapping. 'Queen Latifah' is a stage name, chosen in order to signify greatness and to create an image suggesting maternal lineage and kinship with the unknown Queens of Africa. Thus, Latifah chose a name which conforms to the male-defined stereotype of 'what women should be'. In combining the name Latifah with her self-appointed monarchy under the title of Queen, she subverts expectation in actual as well as symbolic terms. Latifah's music, like her name, combines serious messages about women's lives with a subversion of expectation. In this sense, it operates in a similar way to the women's stand-up comedy discussed in Article 6.1.

One last point can be made about Queen Latifah's name. It has symbolic significance, as do many words in spoken and written language. The word 'Queen' is gender specific, as is the word 'ladies' in the song referred to above. Both words are used self-consciously, as strategies for making statements by subverting expectations about the images normally associated with words. You need only think of the Queen Mother, or of a Victorian Lady, to see the striking difference between those images and the image created and projected by Queen Latifah. Thus, as in discussion of women's language in Chapter 1, and in discussion of gendered language and writing in Chapter 2, it is important in this part of the course to understand that some words and phrases are used in gender-specific ways. In comedy, the standard images and expectations associated with words are often subverted, or overturned, to comic effect.

There are several ways in which what you have learned about language and communication in earlier parts of the course are relevant to the treatment of comic language in this part. For instance, in Radio Programme 09 Sara Maitland talked about the derivation of the word 'gossip': a word which originally had religious connotations associated with childbirth and taking responsibility for children, but which has evolved as a gendered term most often associated with talkative women. The word is not inherently negative, nor inherently female, though it is often interpreted as both. Similarly, Meagan Morris's discussion of nagging as a powerless discourse (quoted and discussed in Article 6.1) points out that it is not what is said in a 'nag' which makes it negative, but rather the context in which the 'nag' is uttered, and the way in which it is ignored and therefore repeated. Nagging and gossiping are generally viewed as women's ways of communicating. But comediennes, musicians, poets, writers and critics who 'take the mike', or the pen, and speak for themselves have found that there are other ways of communicating, some of which are enjoyable as well as politically and personally effective.

CHAPTER 6 COMIC SUBVERSIONS

Figure 19
Queen Latifah. Photograph by Jayne Wexler

ARTICLE 6.2 'COMIC SUBVERSIONS: COMEDY AS STRATEGY IN FEMINIST THEATRE' BY LIZBETH GOODMAN

You should now read Article 6.2 (pp. 301–320), making a note of key themes and ideas as you do so.

Three main ideas are raised in this article, and the first two have already been discussed at length (they are: the relationship between role playing in everyday life and on stage; and the potential for comedy to make serious feminist points, as well as to entertain). The third idea is the importance of audience reception and interpretation. The audience of the theatre event is emphasized in this article, when Goodman writes (on pp. 301–302) that:

> The female majority in most theatre audiences also influences interpretation and reception by enriching the (gendered) dynamic between stage and world which is the context of any play in performance. This article argues that the gendered dynamic between the audience and the performance has particular implications for plays by and about women.

You may recall that this was also a key issue discussed in the introduction to *Imagining Women*, where, on page 1, Bonner and Goodman wrote:

> Most of the articles in this book could be described as examples of feminist cultural studies. They are concerned with the processes of production, dissemination and consumption of texts; they ask questions about how audiences (and particularly female audiences) use texts, how meaning is made from them and how they are incorporated into everyday life. There is also a special concern with how they evolve and grow *from* everyday life.

This last article on feminist comic theatre was, again, not intended to raise new issues, but rather to represent the key ideas of the book in a different light. Radio Programme 10, *Feminist Theatre*, enriches this part of your study with extracts from a play in performance: Bryony Lavery's *Her Aching Heart*. The issues and ideas raised in Article 6.2 and in Radio 10 are quite similar. In both, as in Book Four and the course as a whole, your role as a reader involves reception, critical thought and interpretation, as well as comparison with personal experience and evaluation in terms of the value of new ideas in relation to your own life.

SUMMARY

There is one thing which you no doubt noticed immediately when you first looked over the contents of this part of *Imagining Women*. Indeed, after spending so much time considering the implications of authorship and positionality, it would be difficult not to notice that this part of *Imagining Women* was written by a single author. As this is the only part of the book with a single author, it is worth asking (and answering) a few rhetorical questions about Chapter 6 as a whole.

What are the implications of single authorship in terms of the style and the bias or perspective of the material? Well, you may notice that the style is fairly consistent throughout. Yet it might have been handled differently if, for instance, the first and second articles had been written by different authors. But it is certain aspects of the positionality of these two articles which are most important in the context of your study. The positionality of the author in terms of age, race and class might have influenced the choice of comediennes interviewed, but this was avoided in the effort to include women from a range of ages, ethnic origins and class positions. Similarly, the focus on lesbian comedy in the second article was intended to ensure the representation of both lesbian and heterosexual women in this larger discussion of 'comic subversions'.

In this chapter, as in all of *Imagining Women* and in the course as a whole, we have stressed a few key themes and ideas. These are:

- The benefits of hearing women's voices.
- The importance of seeing women's self-representations in all kinds of different media.
- The significance of women as the subjects of our study.
- The contribution of women's studies to women's and men's lives.

These ideas are addressed in the conclusion to *Imagining Women*, which is Alice Walker's 'In Search of Our Mothers' Gardens'.

> If you have not already done so, read the piece by Alice Walker (pp. 321–329) now, before moving on to the last section of this Study Guide.

8
BOOK FOUR CONCLUSION
(SECOND HALF OF WEEK 30)
(prepared by Lizbeth Goodman)

The conclusion to *Imagining Women* is Alice Walker's 'In Search of Our Mothers' Gardens'. We have not introduced this in the text itself: it stands on its own as a literary critical essay which describes the significance of one woman's imaginings of self as a woman in society.

You might wonder why we chose a piece of autobiographical fiction to conclude our book, rather than a piece of 'teaching prose'. The answer is related to the title of the book: *Imagining Women*. We want you to make the final connections yourself. These connections will be individual as well as collective. Yours will be slightly different from your friends' or your tutor's.

You have been provided with a Course Conclusion which lists key points for review and suggests ways in which you might reframe and compare some of the ideas raised in the course. We decided not to provide a similar conclusion for *Imagining Women*. Partly, this is because we wanted the Course Conclusion to serve this function. But also, it was because at this point we want you to add your own voice to those you have heard (read, seen, thought about, experienced) throughout this book and the course.

Having read and thought about the relevance of 'In Search of Our Mothers' Gardens' to *Imagining Women* and the course as a whole, take some time – before you move on to the Course Conclusion – to ask yourself why, in addition to the reasons given above, the course team might have chosen this piece by Walker rather than a more 'academic' piece, or rather than writing a conclusion ourselves.

Again, this is a hypothetical question. We provided this piece because it opens up the issues raised in this book, rather than closing them off in an artificially rounded way. This reading requires you to engage on a personal as well as an academic level. The following activities have therefore been designed to help integrate Walker's piece into your experience of reading *Imagining Women*, rather than vice versa. They have also been designed to help you to tie together the themes of this block, and to relate the work you have done in the past seven weeks to the rest of the course. The activities are optional and need not be done straight away – but if you have time, you might like to do them now. Alternatively, they could be used as revision exercises at the end of the course. They are meant to be enjoyable as well as educational; they are meant to 'put you in the picture'. All are based on the ideas raised in Alice Walker's essay, so if you do these exercises at some point in the future, you might want to review 'In Search of Our Mothers' Gardens' as well.

► **ACTIVITY 49** ◄

Do you and your mother (or other significant older woman in your life) 'speak the same language'? Why or why not? Answer in terms of the ways in which education and personal experience have made your life different from hers, and thereby influenced your ways of seeing and of communicating.

► **ACTIVITY 50** ◄

At some point in your life, you have probably been given something by your mother (or some other significant older woman in your life) which was given to her by someone else. This may have been a physical object (a family heirloom such as a photograph, a piece of jewellery, a bit of lace) or it may have been something intangible (a story about your ancestors, information about your origins, a statement of personal philosophy which has influenced your way of seeing things). Think back to this gift. What was it? When and why was it given? Picture or imagine this gift, whatever it was, and then imagine the woman who gave it. Ask yourself whether you will pass it on in time to someone else: a daughter, niece or friend. Record your thoughts on this.

► **ACTIVITY 51** ◄

Think back to the quilt described in Alice Walker's 'In Search of our Mothers' Gardens'. In what ways can that quilt be thought of as an heirloom, a gift, from all women to you and to everyone who sees, reads or hears about it? Make a note of your answers.

ACTIVITY 52

Alice Walker describes the quilt in 'In Search of our Mothers' Gardens' as having been made of 'bits and pieces of worthless rags ... the only materials she could afford' (p. 326). In what ways can that quilt be thought of as a form of autobiography? Again, make a note of your answers.

When you have had a chance to think through your responses to these activities, you will have addressed some of the key points of *Imagining Women* and the fourth and last block of your course.

POETRY SUPPLEMENT

Before moving on to the final part of your study, there is one last activity (in six parts) appended to the Poetry Supplement, which has been designed to help unify the many ideas and themes which have been raised in *Imagining Women* and in the course as a whole.

> Turn now to the Poetry Supplement, read it through and do the activity which appears at the end.

Before leaving Book Four and this Study Guide, take a few minutes to reflect on all the various forms of representations you have encountered in your study of *Imagining Women*. We hope you will see that the forms of representations discussed are all part of the fabric of our daily lives: that the representation of and by women is not only an academic subject for 'issues in women's studies', but also a real issue for each of us.

Some of you may wish to do further research in various issues in women's studies when you have completed this course. We have therefore provided a list of suggestions for further reading which may be of assistance. This is produced in the form of a Stop Press, which you should have received by now. We chose the Stop Press format as it allows us to update and extend the list when new books become available. And of course, it is important that the suggestions are taken *as* suggestions: they are not necessary for this course. Indeed, it would not be advisable for you to try to do any more reading at this point. Rather, the suggestions may be of interest to those of you wishing to continue your studies after completing this course.

Some of the issues in women's studies we have looked at in Book Four and this Study Guide are reviewed and summarized in the Course Conclusion.

REFERENCES

ADAMS, M.J. (n.d.) 'The Harriet Powers pictorial quilts', *Black Art*, vol. 3, no. 4, pp. 12–28.

BARR, R. (1990) *My Life as a Woman*, London, Fontana.

BROWN, M.E. (1990) 'Motley moments: soap opera, carnival, gossip and the power of the utterance', in Brown, M.E. (ed.) *Television and Women's Culture: the politics of the popular*, London, Sage, pp. 193–4.

CARTER, A. (ed.) (1986) *Wayward Girls and Wicked Women: an anthology of stories*, London, Virago.

CHESTER, G. and NIELSON, S. (eds) (1987) *In Other Words: writing as a feminist*, London, Century Hutchinson.

FRASER, J. and BOFFIN, T. (1991) *Stolen Glances: lesbians take photographs*, London, Pandora Press.

FREEMAN, J. (1990) *Oral History*, Autumn issue: The Crafts, pp. 27–8.

GILBERT, S. and GUBAR, S. (1979) *The Madwoman in the Attic: a study of women and the literary imagination in the nineteenth century*, New Haven, CT, Yale University Press.

HAYTHORNE, E. (1990) *On Earth to Make the Numbers Up*, Castleford, Yorkshire Art Circus.

HOBSON, D. (1990) 'Women audiences and the workplace', in Brown, M.E. (ed.) *Television and Women's Culture: the politics of the popular*, London, Sage, p. 65.

JOUVE, W.N. (1991) *White Woman Speaks With Forked Tongue: criticism as autobiography*, London, Routledge.

MOERS, E. (1978) *Literary Women*, London, The Women's Press.

SHOWALTER, E. (ed.) (1985) *The New Feminist Criticism: essays on women, literature and theory*, New York, Pantheon.

SULTER, M. (ed.) (1990) *Passion: discourses on blackwomen's creativity*, Hebden Bridge, Urban Fox Press.

TULLOCH, J. (1990) *Television Drama: agency, audience and myth*, London, Routledge.

ACKNOWLEDGEMENTS

Grateful acknowledgement is made to the following sources for permission to reproduce material in this Study Guide:

Text

Mackenzie. S. (1991), 'Free verse', *The Guardian*, 16 October 1991; Norman, G. (1991), 'Artist gives magazine a line on raising cash', *The Independent*, 18 April 1991; Freeman, J. (1990), 'The crafts (Quilting)', *Oral History*, Autumn 1990, University of Essex, Department of Sociology, Oral History Society, Wivenhoe Park, Colchester, CO4 3SQ; Reed, C. (1990), 'Second class superstars', *The Guardian*, 22 November 1990; Lyrics from 'Ladies first' by Queen Latifah, (1989). Courtesy of Tommy Boy Music Inc., New York; Extracts from Feminists Against Censorship leaflet 'Ask yourself ... do you really want more censorship?', Summer 1989. Reproduced by permission of Feminists Against Censorship, 38 Mount Pleasant, London, WC1X 0BP.

Illustrations

Figure 1: Edouard Manet *Le Déjeuner sur l'Herbe (The Picnic)*, 1863, oil on canvas, 208 x 264 cm., Musée d'Orsay, Paris. Photo: Réunion des Musées Nationaux Documentation Photographique; *Figure 2: Blasphemy.* Photography by Jean Fraser from *Celestial Bodies*, in *Stolen Glances*, edited by Tessa Boffin and Jean Fraser, 1991, London, Pandora Press; *Figure 3:* James Caan and Kathy Bates in *Misery*, 1990. Photograph: John Kobal Collection; *Figure 4:* Glenn Close, Michael

Douglas, Anne Archer in *Fatal Attraction*, 1987. Photograph: John Kobal Collection; *Figure 5:* Meryl Streep, Roseanne Barr and Ed Begley Jnr in *The She-Devil*, 1989. Photograph: John Kobal Collection; *Figure 6:* Grace Nichols. Photograph: *The Guardian*/Graham Turner; *Figure 8:* 'Artist gives magazine a line on raising cash' by Geraldine Norman, *The Independent*, 18 April 1991; *Figure 9:* Edouard Manet, *A Bar at the Folies Bergère*, 1881–2, 95 x 130 cm. Courtauld Institute Galleries, London, Courtauld gift 1934; *Figure 10:* 'Give her your pay packet'. Photograph by Jill Posener, London 1982; *Figure 11:* Mrs Lough, well-known Durham quilter. Photograph: The North of England Open Air Museum, Beamish, County Durham; *Figure 12:* Plaiting, photographic sequence from Yemi Morgan 'In the Shade of the Avocado Tree, the Girl Next Door and Me', in *Passion: discourses on blackwomen's creativity*, edited by Maud Sulter, 1990, Hebden Bridge, Urban Fox Press, ISBN 1-872124 30 5 (hbk), 1-872124 31 3 (pbk). Photograph: Ingrid Pollard; *Figure 13:* Sharon Gless and Tyne Daly in *Cagney and Lacey*. Photograph: John Kobal Collection; *Figure 14:* Madonna in performance. Photograph: London Features International/Billy Bong; *Figure 15:* Cover of Roseanne Barr, *Roseanne, My Life as a Woman*, 1990, London, Fontana/Collins. Reproduced by permission of HarperCollins Ltd; *Figure 16:* Spare Tyre. Photograph: Ute Klaphake, courtesy of Spare Tyre Theatre Company; *Figure 17:* Donna and Kebab in *Acropolis Now*, Assembly Hall, Edinburgh, August–September 1991. Photograph: Xenia Demetriou; *Figure 18:* Sheila Hyde. Photograph by courtesy of Equity; *Figure 19:* Queen Latifah. Photograph by Jayne Wexler; *p. 37:* 'Your fiction demeans', cartoon by David Austin, *New Scientist*, 4 August 1990, by permission of the artist; *p. 97:* Les Gibbard, cartoon drawn after the May 1979 General Election but not published until later in *Weekend Guardian*, 19–20 October 1991. Reproduced by permission of the artist; *pp. 97–98:* cartoons from *Trouble and Strife*, no. 11, Summer 1987: (a) 'A woman's right to choose', cartoon by Cath Jackson; (b) 'Information is power', cartoon by Angela Martin; (c) 'What is Good feminist practice', cartoon by Angela Martin; (d) 'Why are very supportive environments very unsupported financially', cartoon by Angela Martin.